HUMAN RIGHTS EDUCATION
Theory and Practice

HUMAN RIGHTS EDUCATION
Theory and Practice

C. Naseema

SHIPRA

(First Published in India in 2008)

Rs. 995, US$ 49.75

ISBN: 978-81-7541-391-7

2017 Impression

Human Rights Education: Theory and Practice

Published by:

SHIPRA PUBLICATIONS
LG 18-19, Pankaj Central Market,
I.P. Ext., Patparganj, Delhi 110092, India
Ph.: +91 11 22236152, 9650028065, 9810522367
Email: info@shiprapublication.com
Website: www.shiprapublication.com

Foreword

It is indeed admirable to find a teacher in the Faculty of Education devoting time and effort to study the principles and practice of Human Rights and then writing a book to educate others on this essential knowledge of empowerment and dignity. At a time when the legal community is not doing enough on human rights education and a vast section of Indian humanity are still ignorant of their rights and entitlements, this young crusader has come forward to do her bit for the cause of justice and good governace through her creative work on the subject. I congratulate Dr. C. Naseema and all those who encouraged her including the University of Calicut, the U.G.C. and a host of secondary schools who worked under her guidance.

The book is imaginatively organized, the first part introducing the idea of human rights to the lay readers in non-technical language and the second part providing instructional tools on easy teaching/ learning of the essence of human rights. Of course, the author has given a wide meaning to the concept by discussing many ordinary legal rights as well. After all, the object is to introduce rights jurisprudence in the discourse at the school level and to inculcate in the young minds a healthy interest on rights and duties to sustain liberal democratic values towards developing a human rights culture in society. There is due emphasis on teaching methods which can be used even outside the formal school system.

What is distinctive of the book is the contents of the second part in which teaching modules in multiple languages are provided through simple story-telling style. Each module carry learning objectives and teaching guidelines. Though I did not have the benefit of reading the entire manuscript, I could get the message designed to the needs of the students in the Science and Humanities streams. This is a remarkable venture and the author's expertise in educational psychology is reflected in it.

I had occasion to meet Dr. C. Naseema only once several years ago in a human rights seminar in Bangalore. I am glad to say that she continued her interest in human rights education and now has made a significant contribution in the dissemination of the knowledge she has acquired over the years. I wish her all success in her future endeavours in this direction and recommend her work for use in schools in Kerala and outside.

Padmasree Prof. N.R. Madhava Menon

Devi Priya
Trivandrum

Preface

Human rights are not merely a language of compassion, co-operation and communication, but a grammar of civilized society and an essential condition of a happy, peaceful and prosperous future. So, the greatest challenge before us is to ensure an equitable distribution of human rights.

Hearing some criticism of human rights by some international agencies, India passed a Protection of Human Rights Act under which National Human Rights Commission under the chairmanship of former Chief Justice of India Sri. Ranganath Misra was constituted. In its annual report of 1994-95, the commission has recommended wide ranging reforms for the protection of human rights.

The need for human rights education has been emphasised in the UDHR and other international documents and treaties. The human rights education consists of efforts to build a universal culture of human rights through the imparting of knowledge and skills and moulding attitudes.

The human rights education can both help to reduce human rights violations and contribute to building free, and peaceful societies. Human rights should be a subject to all levels of education. The book aims to present a general overview of the human rights and the implementation of human rights education. Also the Pedagogical aspects of Human Rights Education is included.

The book deals specifically with a detailed coverage of human rights in general, special rights such as right to Development, right to Environment, right to Information, Intellectual property rights and Consumer rights, implementation of human rights and human rights education in India, methods and activities the teachers can use in classrooms for teaching human rights, role of teacher educators, problems faced by teachers of human rights, and implementation of human rights education at elementary, secondary, higher secondary levels, activities which teachers can use in teaching human rights.

I acknowledge U.G.C. for sanctioning me a Major Research Project on human rights education which helped me to go in depth of the Human Rights Education. So, I express wholehearted gratitude to the University Grants Commission.

I am taking this opportunity to record my sincere gratitude to Prof. Syed Iqbal Hasnain for his encouragement and help to complete the major research project in Human Rights Education.

The book is the product of a series of workshops conducted on Human Rights Education for the preparation of Modules for incorporating Human Rights Education in the existing secondary school curriculum of Kerala State. I am thankful to Adv. M.P. Shyjal, Prof. N.P. Hafiz Mohamed, Prof. P. Sreedharan, Dr. G. Balraj for giving their expertise in helping the secondary school teachers for preparing the modules.

I am much thankful to Dr. P.K. Abdul Gafoor, A. Rajendran, Rajasekharan Unni, M. Thamban, Velayudhan. K. P, V.M. GopalaKrishnan, Ramakrishnan, Ambily. G, K.G. Radha, Dr. V. Usha, Beena N. Kurup, Mrs. N.J. Aleese, M.A.George, Vinod Kumar. K, Abdurahiman. N, who lead the team of teachers for the preparation of modules in each subject.

It is hoped that this book will be useful to the students, teachers, prospective teachers and teacher educators and all others who are concerned with human rights education.

March 2007

Dr. C. Naseema
Head, Dept. of Education
University of Calicut

Contents

1

Introduction

Human rights are, literally, the rights that one has simply because one is a human being.

The nature has bestowed man with two related characteristics-first as an individual and then as a social being. Living in a group organized community is natural to him. To understand human rights, one must look through their history, which will take us back to the day when man first started living in groups. It was natural that many instances might have prevailed over what was right; those who held power dominated the weak.

With the passage of time, these rights or established customs or understandings including the relationship between the ruler and the ruled were brought together in different forms, in various parts of the world. As a result of the convergence of several historical factors, a concept of human rights emerged by the middle of the present century. This development found expression in the Charter of the United Nations-which proclaimed "universal respect for, and observance of, human rights and Fundamental freedom for all without distinctions as to race, sex, language or religion." The Charter made promotion of thcsc rights as onc of its basic purposes and obligated member states "to take joint and separate action in cooperation with the United Nations for the achievement of this purpose." Thus human rights were being universalised and internationalised. UN charter has laid down principles of a general nature. Human rights are not defined or specified in this Charter.

There arises the necessity to define human rights and fundamental freedom so that the objectives of the Charter could be pursued and an international system, for the promotion and protection of human rights could be instituted. Hence in December 1948, the UN General Assembly proclaimed the Universal Declaration of Human Rights. It defines specific rights-civil and political as well as economic, social and cultural-with equality and freedom from discrimination as a principal and recurrent theme. The Universal Declaration was not conceived as law but as a "common standard of achievement" for all people and all nations.

The Declaration carries no legal sanction to compel states to meet the obligation of ensuring observance and implementation of human rights enshrined in the Declaration. To seek such a legal framework and to convert the norms set in the Declaration into legally binding obligations, efforts were directed, beginning in1947. After 20 years of preparatory work, the General Assembly promulgated International Covenants in December 1966, comprising three instruments as follows:

(*i*) International Covenants on Economic, Social and Cultural Rights.
(*ii*) International Covenants on Civil and Political Rights and
(*iii*) Optional Protocol (on individual petition) to the covenants on civil and Political Rights

The covenants have assumed a prime place in international law as the instruments that influence and at the same time judge the disregard of States and by which the conditions of individual rights in particular countries are to be assessed.

HUMAN RIGHTS — MEANING

"Right" in English, like equivalent words in several other languages, has two central moral and political senses: rectitude and entitlement.

In the sense of rectitude, we speak of "the right thing to do," of *something being* right (or wrong). In the narrower sense of entitlement, we typically speak of *someone having* a right.

Rectitude and entitlement both link "right" and obligation, but in systematically different ways. Claims of rectitude (righteousness)—"That's wrong," "That's not right," "You really ought to do that"—focus on a standard of conduct and draw attention to the duty-bearer's obligation under that standard. Rights claims, by contrast, focus on the right-holder and draw the duty-bearer's attention to the right-holder's special title to enjoy her right.

Human rights are *equal* rights: one either is or is not a human being, and therefore has the same human rights as everyone else (or none at all). They are also *inalienable* rights: one cannot stop being human, no matter how badly one behaves nor how barbarously one is treated. And they are *universal* rights, in the sense that today we consider all members of the species *Homo sapiens* "human beings," and thus holders of human rights.

Every individual has dignity. The principles of human rights were drawn up by human beings as a way of ensuring that the dignity of everyone is properly and equally respected, that is, to ensure that a human being will be able to fully develop and use human qualities such as intelligence, talent and conscience and satisfy his or her spiritual and other needs.

Dignity gives an individual a sense of value and worth. The existence of human rights demonstrates that human beings are aware of each other's worth. Human dignity is not an individual, exclusive and isolated sense. It is a part of our common humanity.

Human rights enable us to respect each other and live with each other. In other words, they are not only rights to be requested or demanded but rights to be respected and be responsible for. The rights that apply to you also apply to others.

The denial of human rights and fundamental freedoms not only is an individual and personal tragedy, but also creates conditions of social and political unrest, sowing the seeds of violence and conflict within and between societies and nations.

Basically, human rights are the claims of the individual for such conditions as are essential for the fullest realization of the innate characteristics which nature has bestowed him/ her with as a human being. It implies that there are inherent and inalienable rights which are due to an individual by virtue of his/her being a human being and that they are necessary to ensure the dignity of every person as a human being irrespective of one's race, religion, nationality, language, sex, or any other factor.

All "claims" of the individual, for example, freedom to live as one wishes to or to do whatever one wants to do, cannot be treated as human rights. Only those claims which are essential for the developments of one's personality and recognized as such by the "society" constitute rights. But one has to recognize the fact that this idea is not the reality and that what is conceptually recognized as idea of freedom and equality. It is not possible to project a new institution upon social relation which have been superseded, and to which it does not correspond. In order for human rights to appear as the general rule in society, and for them to be felt both as a need and as a reality, it was indispensable for there to be basic social changes in the relations of production (more precisely, in the relations of ownership) within the previous social system-feudalism. Everyone's rights had to be recognised as being, in principle, equal with regard to ownership and the acquisition and enjoyment of property.

The right to property had previously been regarded as a natural right or in other words as a fundamental and inalienable right of man, first by Aquinas, then later more explicitly by Grotius, who set this right outside the universe of natural rights. Grotius had asserted that the right to property had been "introduced by human will" and so that we should not be offended. He invited us to understand and to consider our property as corresponding to natural law.

Two major ideas emerged from this line of reasoning, but both subsequently splintered off from this origin. They were the ideas of freedom and equality. The idea of freedom was that of free ownership, of the free possession of property and to this was later added the idea of free enterprise, with all other corollaries of freedom.

As for the idea of equality, it too owes its origin, to the appearance of a new type of ownership. It signified equality for all as regards the right to acquire property. But considering more closely its true origin turns out too be connected with the political idea of the state in the modern sense of the term. It also concerned equality in respect of participation in political life. Consequently, equality was, a political idea and a political right, whereas freedom possessed an economic character, at least so far as its origins were concerned.

According to modern political philosophy, every individual should possess equal rights in the life of the State. Subsequently the notion of equality was made to apply to the whole of man, too all of man's abilities and all of his rights. However, an important difference was to remain between freedom and equality-bound up with ownership, freedom was considered to be a right which the State would not restrict because it was an absolute right. This was not true of equality as it was regarded as a political right and, as such, it could be restricted by the State.

(*b*) Origins at the Level of Positive Law

The origins of human rights, in respect of positive law, are traced back to documents which appeared in recent centuries. According to this point of view human rights are contracts concluded by the State with the population and, first of all, with the mobility. These contracts are seen as preserving certain rights for men while preventing the State from interfering in the exercise of those rights. The legal force of these rights is seen as being founded (contrary to the conception of the theory of the contract founded on natural law) on the will of the State, or better still, in the circumstances of the period, on their recognition by the King.

The fact that human rights on agreements with a similar objective in view have been given the form of Charters, Bills or Petitions and, where appropriate, Declarations, has led to these documents being placed on the same theoretical footing, although they were produced at different periods and for different purposes. In particular, in the specialized literature, a whole discussion is to be found on the common or different nature of the Magna Carta, the Petition of Rights and the Bill of Rights, as well as of the Declaration of Virginia and the Bills which followed it, and the French Declaration of 1789.

In Central Europe, George Jellinek's book on the declaration of human rights (1904) caused a turmoil by subscribing to the view that the documents—i.e., Magna Carta, the Petition of Rights and the Bills of Rights as well as the Declaration of Virginia and the Bills which followed it and the French Declaration of 1789—followed on from each other and were consequently directly related to each other. Moreover, he was not the only one who expressed that opinion.

Jellinek found it necessary to observe, in the second edition of his book, that in United States the Bill of Rights has represented the culminating point, whereas the French Declaration was the starting point, which in itself constitutes a radical difference. Jellinek indirectly acknowledges, at the level of the history of civilization and of philosophy, as well as from the social point of view, the importance of the Declaration adopted by the Constituent Assembly of 1789. The starting point of human rights in the modern sense of the term is clearly to be found both in the 'Declaration of the Rights of Man and of the Citizen', voted during the French Revolution, and in the social conditions underlying it.

(*c*) Conceptions based on 'Natural Law'

According to the most traditional conception of human rights, at the time that men passed from the primitive state to the social state they concluded a contract between themselves, and by this contract they renounced part of their natural rights, which they had enjoyed in their free state, while preserving certain basic rights: the right to life, freedom and equality. The rights thus preserved constituted eternal and inalienable rights that every social and State system was obliged to respect.

As for the origin of these rights, there are various differences to be found in the way in which the conception founded on natural law is set forth. The theory of the social contract is the product of the school of natural law which made its appearance in the 15th and 16th centuries. According to this school, human rights are bound up with man's basic nature from which they derive, and for which reason they constitute human rights.

According to another conception, which goes back to Locke, the starting point was tolerance in respect of their religions or, in other words, right to profess any religion. Again, what is involved is a conception referring to natural law. Furthermore, this idea set the scene for the creation of the United States of America, considering that freedom of religion played an important part in this connection.

There exists other conceptions of human rights, for instance that according to which human rights originated in human understanding. Conceptions of this kind were already subscribed to the Middle Ages. Virtually all the feudal varieties of the natural law theory belong to this type of thinking, and the same is true of the Kantian theory of law, founded on reason. This theory, like all others is forced to start off from certain promises established a *priori* and from which it is possible to deduce human rights.

(*d*) The Rights of Man and of the Citizen

The French Declaration of the Rights of Man and of the Citizen of 1789 and other documents which appeared subsequently, made a distinction between the rights of man and, on the other, rights of the citizen. Man in these texts appears as a being who is imagined to exist outside society, who is assumed to exist prior to society. As for the citizen, he is subject to the State's authority. On this account, the rights of man are natural and inalienable rights, while the rights of the citizen are positive rights, rights granted by the positive law.

In the course of social, political and ideological development, this hierarchy in respect of the appearance and existence of the rights of man and of the citizen has, to certain extent, become blurred. As the distinctions between the rights of man and the rights of the citizen has disappeared, the two categories have merged. In so far as certain traces of this distinction have remained, it has assumed new forms and has come to appear as a criterion for differentiating between branches of law. All rights as a whole which are recognized by constitutions are thus considered as belonging to the category of the rights of the citizen, wherever the rights of man are those covered by international law.

Like this, the problem of human rights has been entirely reduced to the question of the simple relationship between two branches of law, a relationship in which constitutional law seems to be subordinate to international law.

(*e*) Constitutional Law

In national systems human rights re-appear in the form of citizen's rights in constitutional law. It is in the constitutions that human rights are established. For example, the French Constitution of 1791, the text of which is preceded by the Declaration of the Rights of man and of the citizen of 1789. The constitutions which followed no longer provide a general formulation of these rights in their preambles but integrate them into the actual text as basic rights upon which the State is founded. These rights determine the relations between the State and the citizen and define the domain in which the State does not intercede.

At the same time, human rights become affected by a specific bias in constitutional law in that they acquire a particular character, linked up with the State's internal structure. The various constitutions, strange to say, omit-to define- the effect of the rights listed. They do not explicitly state which of these rights have a direct effect on the basic of Constitutional law, and which ones necessitates special laws in order for them to be put into effect. Consequently, fundamental rights are provisions binding solely upon the legislature and are of no benefit to citizens except by this indirect channel.

In the socialist countries, there are different views as to the place that the citizen's fundamental rights should occupy in the constitution-whether they should be formulated ahead of constitutional law or, on the contrary, be included in the actual text of the constitution.

In constitution law, there is a mixture of human rights and citizen's rights. It falls to theory to re-establish the notion of human rights and to set them back in their place. In practice, constitutions contain a hierarchical system of citizen's rights which constitutes the starting point of the system of human rights as it has been formulated by international law.

HUMAN RIGHTS GUARANTEED IN MAIN INTERNATIONAL TREATIES

1. Right to a nationality
2. Right to work
3. Right to food
4. Right to social security
5. Right to enjoy the highest standards of physical and mental health
6. Right to education
7. Right to participation in cultural life
8. Right to environment
9. Right for development
10. Intellectual property rights
11. Right of the child
12. Right of women
13. Right to life
14. Right to self determination
15. Right to Non-discrimination
16. Right to for prohibition of Apartheid
17. Right to prohibition of retroactivity for criminal offences
18. Right to prohibition of imprisonment for contractual obligation
19. Right to procedural guarantee in criminal trials
20. Right to physical and moral integrity
21. Prohibition of torture and of cruel, inhuman or degrading treatment or punishment
22. Right to prohibition of slavery, of forced labour and of trafficking in persons.
23. Right to recognition of legal personality
24. Right to liberty and security

25. Prohibition of arbitrary arrest, detention, and exile
26. Right to freedom of movement and residence
27. Right to seek asylum
28. Right to privacy
29. Right to freedom of thought, conscience, and religion
30. Right to freedom of expression
31. Right to freedom of peaceful assembly
32. Right to freedom of association
33. Right to marry and to found a family
34. Right to protection of motherhood and childhood

2

Human Rights in Indian Condition

INDIAN CONSTITUTION AND HUMAN RIGHTS

The establishment of a democratic and secular political system and the reconstruction and modernising of society on the principles of egalitarianism and respect for India's cultural diversity were central to the vision of independence struggle. In 1931, the Indian National Congress adopted a resolution on Fundamental Rights and Economic Programme. This resolution expressed solidarity with anti colonial struggles and movements of social progress and democracy in other countries and with the victims of fascist agrarian.

The constitution of the Republic of India, which came into force on 26th January, 1950 with 395 article and nine schedules is one of the most elaborate fundamental laws ever adopted. The preamble to the constitution pledges to secure to all the citizens of India,

Justice—Social, economic ad political

Liberty—of though, expression, behalf, faith and worship

Equality—of status and opportunity and Fraternity, assuring the dignity of the individual and the unity and integrity of the nation

CONSTITUTIONAL PROVISIONS OF HUMAN RIGHTS

Two parts of the constitution embody most human rights, distinguishing between judicially enforceable fundamentals rights and rights not so enforceable, namely Part III and Part IV. The details are given below.

PART- III
FUNDAMENTAL RIGHTS

General

Article 12: *Definition-* In their part, unless the context otherwise requires, "the State" includes the Government and Parliament of India and the Government and Legislature of each of the states and all local or other authorities within the territory of the India or under the control of the Government of India.

Article 13: *Laws inconsistent with or derogation of the fundamental rights—*

(1) All laws in force in the territory of India immediately before the commencement of their Constitution, in so far as they are inconsistent with the processions of this Part, shall, to the extent of such inconsistency, be void.

(2) The state shall not make any law which takes away or abridges the rights conferred by their Part and any law made in contravention of this Part and any law made in contravention of this clause shall, to the extent of the contravention, be void.

(3) In this article, unless the context otherwise requires,

(*a*) "Law" includes any ordinance, order, bye-law, rule, regulation, notification, custom or usage having in the territory of India the force of law;

(*b*) "laws in Force' includes laws passed or made by legislature or other competent authority in the territory of India before the commencement of this constitution and not previously replaced not withstanding that any such law or any part thereof may not be then in operation either at all or in particular areas.

(4) Nothing in thus article shall apply to any amendment of their constitution made under Article 368.

[Note: The "basic features" of the constitution cannot be amended by exercising the power of amendment under article 368. The Constitution (42nd Amendment) Act, 1976, which inserted in Article 368 (5) a provision that there is no limitation on the constituent power of the Parliament to amend the constitution, has been invalidated by the Supreme Court adhering to the doctrine of basic features. Though fundamentals rights, as such, are not immune from amendment *en bloc*, particular rights or parts thereof may be held as basic features.]

Article 14: *Equality before law*

The state not deny to any person equality before the law or the equal protection of the laws within the territory of India

Article 15: *Prohibition of discrimination on grounds of religion race, caste, sex, or place of birth*

(1) The state shall not discriminate against any citizen on grounds only religion, race, caste, sex, place of birth or any of them.

(2) No citizen shall, on grounder only of religion, race, caste, sex, place of birth or any of them, be subject to any disability, liability, restriction or condition with regard to

(*a*) Access to shops, public restaurants, hotels and placer of public entertainment or

(*b*) The use of wells, tanks, bathing ghats, roads and places of public resort maintained wholly or party out of state funds or dedicated to the use of the general public.

(3) Nothing in this article shall prevent the state from making any special provision for women and children.

(4) Nothing in this article or in clause (2) of article 29 shall present the state from making any special provision for the advancement of any socially and educationally backward classes of citizens or for the scheduled caster and the scheduled Tribes.

[*Note*: Added by the constitution (first Amendment) Act, 1951, S.2]

Article 16: *Equality of opportunity in matters of employment.*

(1) There shall be equality of opportunity for all citizens in matters relating to employment or appointment to any office under the sate.

(2) No citizen shall, on grounds only of religion, race, caste, sex, descent, place of birth, residence or any of them, be in eligible for, or discriminated against in respect of any employment of office under the state.

(3) Nothing in this article shall prevent Parliament from making any low prescribing, in regard o a class or classes of employment or appointment to an office [under the Government of or any local or

other authority within, a state or union territory, any requirement as to residence within that state or union territory] prior to such employment or appointment.

(4) Nothing in this article shall prevent the state from making any provision for the reservation of appointments or posts in favour of any backward class of citizen which in the opinion of the state, is not adequately represented in the services under the state.

(5) Nothing in this article shall affect the operation of any law which provides that the incumbent of an office in connection with the affairs of any religion or denominational institution or any member of the governing body there of shall be a person professing a particular religion or belonging to a particular denomination.

Article 17: *Abolition of untouchability*

"Untouchability" is abolished and its practice in any form is forbidden. The enforcement of any disability arising out of "Untouchability" shall be an offence punished accordance with the law.

Article 18: *Abolition of titles*

(1) No title, not being a military or academic distinction shall be conferred by the state.

(2) No citizen of India shall accept any title from any foreign state.

(3) No person who is not the citizen of India, shall while he holds any office of profit or trust under the state, accept without the consent of the President any title from any foreign state.

(4) No person holding any office of profit or trust under the state shall without the consent of the President, accept any present, enrolment or office of any kind from or under any foreign state.

Right to Freedom

Article 19: *Protection of Certain Rights Regarding Freedom of Speech etc.*

(1) All citizens shall have the right

(*a*) To freedom of speech and expression.
(*b*) To assemble peaceably and without arms.
(*c*) To form associations or unions.
(*d*) To move freely throughout the territory India (and)
(*e*) To reside and settle in any part of the territory of India (and)

[by the constitution (44th Amendment) Act, 1978, S.2 w.e.f. 20-6-1979]

[sub-clause (*f*) omitted by S.2. Ibid.w.e.f. 20-6-1979].

(*g*) to practise any profession or to carry on any occupation, trade or business.

[(2) Nothing in sub-clause (*a*) of clause (1) shall affect the operation of any existing law, or prevent the state from making any law, in so far as such law imposes reasonable restrictions on the exercise of the right conferred by the said sub-clause in the interests of [2] [the sovereignty and integrity of India the security of the state, friendly relations with foreign states, public order, decency or morality, or in relation to contempt of court, deformation or incitement to an offence]

Note: (1) Subs. By the constitution (First Amendment) Act, 1952, s.3, for cl. (2) with retrospectives effect.

(2) Ins. By the constitution (sixteenth Amendment) Act, 1963, s.2.

(3) Nothing is sub-clause (*b*) of the said clause shall affect the operation of any existing law in so far as it imposes, or prevent the state from making any law imposing, in the interests of [the sovereignty and integrity of India or] public order, reasonable restrictions on the exercise of the right conferred by the said sub-clause.

(4) Nothing is sub-clause (*c*) of the said clause shall affect the operation of any existing law in so far as it imposes, or prevent the state from making any law imposing, in the interests of [the sovereignty and integrity of India or] public order or morality, reasonable restrictions on the exercise of the right conferred by the said sub-clause.

(5) Nothing in [3][sub-clauses (*d*) and (*e*)] of the said clause shall affect the operation of any existing law in so far as it imposes, or prevent the state from making any law imposing, reasonable restrictions on the exercise of any of the rights conferred by the said sub-clauses in the interests of the general public or for the protection of the interests of any scheduled tribe.

[*Note*: (3) Subs by the constitution (forty fourth amendment) Act, 1978, s.2 for "sub-clauses (*d*) to (*f*)" w.e.f. 20-6-1979.

(6) Nothing in sub-clause (*g*) of the said clause shall affect the operation of any existing law in so far as it imposes, or prevents the

state from making any law imposing, in the interests of the general public reasonable restrictions on the exercise of the right conferred by the said sub-clause and in particular, [4][nothing in the said sub-clause shall affect the operation of any existing law in so far as it relates to, or prevent the state from making any law relating to,

(*i*) The professional or technical qualifications necessary for practising any professor or carrying on any occupation, trade or business, or

(*ii*) The carrying on by the state, or by the a corporation owned or controlled by the state, of any trade, business, industry or service, whether, to the exclusion, complete or partial, of citizens [or otherwise]

Note: (4) Subs. By the constitution (First Amendment) Act 1951, S.3, for certain words.

Article 20: *Protection in respect of conviction for offences*

(1) No person shall be convicted of any offence except for violation of a law in force at the time of the commission of the act charged as an offence nor be subjected to penalty greater than that which might have been inflicted under the law in force at the time of the commission of the offence.

(2) No person shall be prosecuted and punished for the same offence more than once.

(3) No person accused of any offence shall be completed to be a witness against himself.

Article 21: *Protection of life and personal liberty*

No person shall be deprived of his life or personal liberty except according to procedure established by law.

Article 22: *Protection against arrest and detention in certain cases*

(1) No person who is arrested shall be detained in custody without being informed, as soon as may be of the grounds for such arrest nor shall be denied the right to consult, and to be defended by a legal practitioner of his choice.

(2) Every person who is arrested and detained in custody shall be produced before the nearest magistrate within a period of twenty-four hours of such arrest excluding the time necessary for the journey from the place of arrest to court of the magistrate and no such person

shall be detained in custody beyond the said period without the authority of a magistrate.

(3) Nothing is clauses (1) and (2) shall apply

(*a*) to any person who for the time being is an enemy alien; or

(*b*) to any person who is arrested or detained under any law providing for preventive detention.

(4) Now law providing for preventive detention shall authorise the detention of a person for a longer period than three months unless

(*a*) an advisory Board consisting of persons who are, or have been, or are qualified to be appointed as, Judges of a High Court has reported before the expiration of the said period of three months that there is in its opinion sufficient cause for such detention:

Provided that nothing in this sub-clause shall authorise the detention of any person beyond the maximum period prescribed by any law made by parliament under sub-clause (b) of clause (7); or

(*b*) Such person is detained in accordance with the provisions of any law made by parliament under sub-clauses (*a*) and (*b*) of clause (7).

(5) When any person is detained in pursuance of an order made under any law providing for preventive detention the authority making the order shall, as soon as may be, communicate to such person the grounds which the order has been made and shall afford hi the earliest opportunity of making a representation against the order.

(6) Nothing in clause (5) shall require the authority making any such order as is referred to in that clause to disclose facts which such authority considers to be against the public interest to disclose.

(7) Parliament may by law prescribe.

(*a*) the circumstances under which and the class or classes in which, a person may be detained for a period longer than three months under any law providing for preventive detention without obtaining the opinion of an advisory board in accordance with the provisions of sub-clause (a) or clause (4);

(*b*) the maximum period for which any person may in any class or classes of cases be detained under any law providing for preventive detention; and (*c*) the procedure to be followed by an advisory board in an inquiry under sub-clause (*a*) of clause (4).

Right Against Exploitation

Article 23: *Prohibition of traffic in human beings and forced labour*

(1) Traffic in human beings and *begar* and other similar forms of forced labour are prohibited and any contravention of their provision shall be an offence punishable in accordance with law.

(2) Nothing in this article shall prevent the state from imposing compulsory service for public purposes and is imposing such service the state shall not make any discrimination on grounds only of religion, race, caste or class or any of them.

Article 24: *Prohibition of employment of children in factories etc.*

No child below the age of fourteen shall be employed to work in any factory, or mine or engaged in any other hazardous employment.

Right to Freedom of Religion

Article 25: *Freedom of Conscious and Free profession practice and propagation of religion.*

(1) Subject to public order, morality and health and the other provisions of their part, all person are equally entitled to freedom of conscience and the freely to profess, practise and propagate religion

(2) Nothing in this article shall affect the operation of any existing law or prevent the state from making any law.

(*a*) regulating or restricting any economic, financial, political or other secular activity which may be associated

(*b*) providing for social welfare and reform or the throwing open of Hindu religious institutions of a public character to all classes and sections of Hindus.

Explanation I –The wearing and carrying of Kripans shall be deemed to be included in the profession of the Sikh religion.

Explanation II–In sub clause (*b*) of clause (2), the reference to Hindus shall be constructed a including a reference to persons professing the Sikh, Jaina or Buddhist religion, and the reference to Hindu religious institutions shall be construed accordingly.

Article 26: *Freedom to manage religious affairs*

Subject to public order, morality and health, every religious denomination or any section thereof shall have the right

(*a*) to establish and maintain institutions for religious and charitable purposes.

(*b*) To manage its own affairs in matters of religion.

(*c*) To own and acquire movable and immovable property and

(*d*) To administer such property in accordance with law.

Article 27: *Freedom as to payment of taxes for promotion of any particular religion*

No person shall be compelled to pay any taxes, the proceeds of which are specifically appropriated in payment of expenses for the promotion on maintenance of any particular religion or religious denomination.

Article 28: *Freedom as to attendance at religious instructions or religious worship in certain educational institutions.*

(1) no religious instruction shall be provided in any educational institution wholly maintained out of state funds.

(2) Nothing in clause (1) shall apply to an educational institution which is administered by the state but has been established under any endowment or trust which requires that religious instruction shall be imparted in such institution.

(3) No person attending any educational institution recognised by the state or receiving aid out of state funds shall be required to take part in any religious instruction that may be imparted in such institution or to attend any religious worship that may be conducted in such institution or in any premises attached there to unless such person or, if such person is a minor, his guardian has given his consent thereto.

Cultural and Educational Rights

Article 29: *Protection of interests of minorities*

Any section of the citizens residing in the territory of India or any part thereof having a distinct language, script or culture of its own shall have the right to conserve the same.

(1) No citizen shall be denied admission into any educational institution maintained by the state of receiving aid out of state funds on grounds only of religion, race, caste, language or any of them.

Article 30: *Right of Minorities to Establish and Administer Educational Institutions*

(1) All minorities, whether based on religion or language, shall have the right to establish and administer educational institutions of their choice.

[1][1(A) In making any law providing for the compulsory acquisition of any property of an educational institution established and administered by a minority, referred to in clause (1), the state shall ensure that the amount fixed by or determined under such law for the acquisition of such property in such as would not restrict or abrogate the right guaranteed under that clause].

(2) The state shall not, in granting aid to educational institutions, discriminate against any educational institution on the ground that it is under the management of a minority, whether based on religion or language.

[Note: (1) Ins. By the construction (44th Amendment) Act 1978, Section 4 (w.e.f 20-6-1979.]

Article 31: [*Compulsory acquisition of property*]

Rep. By the construction (44th Amendment) Act, 1978 S.6 (w.e.f. 20-6-1979)

[1] [Saving of certain Laws]

31A: Saving of Law Providing for Acquisition of Estates, etc.

(1) Not withstanding anything contained in article 13, no law providing for

(*a*) acquisition by the state of any estate or of any rights therein or he extinguishments or modification of any such rights or

(*b*) the taking over of the management of any property by the state for a limited period either in the public interest or in order to secure the proper management of the property, or

(*c*) the amalgamation of two or more corporations either in the public interest or in order to secure the proper management of any of the corporations, or (*d*) the extinguishments or modification of any rights of managing agents, secretaries and treasures, managing directors, directors or managers of corporations, or of any voting rights of shareholders thereof, or

(*e*) the extinguishments or modification of any rights occurring by virtue of any agreement, lease or license for the purpose of searching for, or winning any mineral or mineral oil or the premature term oration or cancellation of any such agreement lease or license, shall be deemed to be void on the ground that it is inconsistent with, or takes away or abridges any of the rights conferred by[2] [article 14 or article 19]

Provided that where such law is a law made by the legislation of a state, the provisions of this article shall not apply thereto unless such law, having been reserved for the consideration of the President, has received his assent.

Provided further that where any law makes any provision for the acquisition by the state of any estate and where any land comprised therein is held by a person under his personal cultivation, it shall not be lawful for the state to acquire any portion of such land as is within the ceiling limit applicable to him under any law for the time being in force or any building or structure standing thereon or appurtenant thereto, unless the law relating to the acquisition of such land, building or structure, provides for payment of compensation at a rate which shall not be less than the market value thereof.

(2) In this Article

(*a*) the expression "estate" shall, in relation to any local area, hence the same meaning or that expression or its local equivalent has in the existing law relating to land tenures in force in that area and shall also include

(*i*) any *Jagir*, *inam* or *muaft* or other similar grant and in the states of [3][Tamil Nadu] and Kerala, any *Janmam* right;

(*ii*) any land held under ryotwari settlement;

(*iii*) any land held or let for purposes of agriculture or for purposes auxiliary thereto, including waste land, forest land, land for posture or sites of buildings and other structures occupied by cultivators of land, agricultural labourers and village artisans.

(*b*) the expression "rights" in relation to an estate shall include any rights vesting in a proprietor, sub-proprietor, under-proprietor, tenure-holder, *rqiyat, under raiyat* or other intermediary and any rights or privileges in respect of land revenue.

[*Note*: (1) Ins. by the constitution (forty-second Amendment] Act, 1976, S.3. w.e.f. 03.01.1977

(2) Subs. by the constitution [44th Amendment] Act, 1978, S.7 for article 14, article 19 or article 31" w.e.f. 20.06.1979.

(3) Subs. by Median state (Alteration of Name) Act, 1968 (53 of 1968), S. 4, for "Madras" w.e.f. 14.01.1969.

31 B. Validation of Certain Acts and Regulations

Without Prejudice to the generality of the provisions contained in article 31 A none of the Acts and Regulations Specified in the Ninth Schedule nor any of the Provisions thereof shall be deemed to be void, or ever to have become void, on the ground that such Act, Regulation or provision inconsistent with, to takes away or abridges any of the rights conferred by, any provisions of this Part, and not withstanding any judgment, decree or order of any court or tribunal to the contrary, each of the said Acts and Regulations shall, subject to the power of any competent legislature to repeal or amend it, continue in force.

31 C. Saving of Laws Giving Effect to Certain Directive Principles

Notwithstanding anything contained in article 13, no law giving effect to the policy of the state towards securing all or any of the principles laid down in Part IV shall be deemed to be void on the ground that it is inconsistent with, or takes away or abridges any of the rights conferred by [1][article 14 or article 19]; and [2]*no law containing a declaration that it is for giving effect to such policy shall be called in question in any court on the ground that it does not give effect to such policy*:

Provided that where such law is made by the Legislature of a state, the processions of this article shall not apply thereto unless such law, having been reserved for the consideration of the President, has received his assent.

[*Note*: (1) Subs. by the constitution (44th Amendment) Act, 1978, S.8 for "article 19 or article 31" w.e.f. 20.06.1979.

(2) In Keshavananda Bharati vs. The state of Kerala (1973). Supp. S. C. R. 1, the Supreme Court held the provisions in italics to be invalid.

31 D. Saving of Laws in Respect of Anti-Natural Activities – Rep. by the Constitution (43rd Amendment) Act, 1977, S. 2 w.e.f. 13.04.1978.

Right to Constitutional Remedies

Article 32: *Remedies for enforcement of rights conferred by this part.*

(1) The right to move the Supreme Court by appropriate proceedings for the enforcement of the rights conferred by this part is guaranteed.

(2) The Supreme Court shall have power to issue directions or orders or writs, including writs in the nature of *habeas corpus, mandamus,* prohibition, *quo warranto* and *certiorari*, whichever may be appropriate, for the enforcement of any of the rights conferred by this part.

(3) Without prejudice to the powers conferred on the Supreme Court by clauses (1) and (2), Parliament may by law empower any other court to exercise within the local limits of its jurisdiction all or any of the powers exercisable by the Supreme Court under clause (2).

(4) The right guaranteed by this article shall not be suspended except as otherwise provided for by this constitution.

[1][Article 33: *Power of Parliament to modify the rights conferred by this part in their application of forces, etc.*

Parliament may, by law, determine to what extent any of the rights conferred by this part shall, in their application to,

(*a*) the members of the Armed Forces; or

(*b*) the members of the Forces charged with the maintenance of public order; or

(*c*) persons employed in any bureau or other organisations established by the state for purpose of intelligence or counter intelligence; or

(*d*) persons employed in, or in connection with the tele-communication systems set up for the purposes of any force; bureau or organisation referred to in clauses (*a*) and (*c*) be restricted or abrogated so as to ensure the proper discharge of the duties and the maintenance of discipline among them.]

[*Note*: (1) Subs. by the constitution (50th Amendment) Act, 1984, S.2 w.e.f. 11.09.1984]

Article 34: *Restriction or rights conferred by this part while martial law is in force in any area*

Notwithstanding anything in the forgoing provisions of this part, parliament may by law indemnify any person in the service of the union or of a state or any connection with the maintenance or restoration of order in any area within the territory of India where martial law was in force or validate any sentence passed, punishment inflicted, forfeiture ordered or other act done under martial law in such area.

Article 35: *Legislation to give effect to the provisions of this part*

Notwithstanding anything in this constitution

(*a*) Parliament shall have, and the Legislature of a state shall not have, power to make laws.

(*i*) with respect to any of the matters which under clause (3) of article 16, clause (3) of article 32, article 33 and article 34 may be provided for by law made by parliament; and

(*ii*) for prescribing punishment for those acts which are declared to be offences under this part, and Parliament shall, as soon as may be after the commencement of this constitution, make laws for prescribing punishment for the acts referred to in sub-clause (*ii*).

(*b*) any law in force immediately before the commencement of this constitution in the territory of India with respect to any of the matters referred to in sub-clause (*i*) of clause (*a*) or providing for punishment for any act referred to in sub-clause (*ii*) of that clause shall, subject to the terms thereof and to any adaptations and modifications that may be made therein under article 372, continue in force until altered or repealed or amended by Parliament.

PART IV
DIRECTIVE PRINCIPLES OF STATE POLICY

Article 36: *Definition:*

In this part, unless the context otherwise requires, "the state" has the same meaning as in Part III.

Article 37: *Application of the principles contained in the is Part*

The provisions contained in this part shall not be enforceable by any court, but the principles therein laid down are nevertheless fundamental in the governance of the country and it shall be the duty of the state to apply these principles in making laws.

Article 38: *State to secure a social order for the promotion of welfare of the people.*

1. [(1) The State shall strive to promote the welfare of the people by securing and protecting as effectively as it may a social order in which justice, social, economic and political, shall inform all the institutions of the national life.

(2) The State shall, in particular, strive to minimise the inequalities in income and endeavour to eliminate inequalities in status, facilities and opportunities, not only amongst individuals but also amongst groups of people residing in different areas or engaged in different vocations.

Article 39. *Certain principles of policy to be followed by the state-the state shall in particular, direct its policy towards securing.*

(*a*) That the citizens, men and women equally, have the right to an adequate means of livelihood;

(*b*) that the ownership and control of the material resources of the community are so distributed as best to sub serve the common good;

(*c*) that the operation of the economic system does nit result in the concentration of wealth and means of production to the common detriment;

(*d*) that there is equal. Pay for equal work for both men and women;

(*e*) that the health and strength of workers, men and women, and the tender age of children are not abused and that citizens are not forced by economic necessity to enter avocations unsuited to their age or strength;

(*f*) that children are given opportunities and facilities to develop in a healthy manner and in conditions of freedom and dignity and that childhood abs youth are protected against exploitation and against moral and material abandonment.

Article 39A. *Equal Justice and free legal aid*

The State shall secure that the operation of the legal system promotes justice, on a basis of equal opportunity, and shall, in particular provide free legal aid, by suitable legislation or schemes or in any other way, to ensure that opportunities for securing justice are not denied to any citizen by reason of economic or other disabilities.

Article 40. *Organisation of village panchayats*

The State shall take steps to organise village panchayats and endow them with such powers and authority as may be necessary to enable them to function as units of self-government.

Note: See the 64th Amendment.

Article 41. *Right to work, to education and to public assistance in certain cases*

The State shall, within the limits of its economic capacity and development, make effective provision for securing the right to work, to education and to pubic assistance in cases of unemployment, old age, sickness and disablement, and in other cases of undeserved want.

Article 42. *Provision for just and humane conditions of work and maternity relief*

The State shall make provision for securing just and humane conditions of work and for maternity relief.

Article 43. *Living wage, etc., for workers*

The State shall endeavour to secure, by suitable legislation or economic organisation or in any other way, to all workers agricultural, industrial or otherwise, work, a living wage, conditions of work ensuring a decent standard of life and full enjoyment of leisure and social and cultural opportunities and, in particular, the State shall endeavour to promote cottage industries on an individual or co-operative basis in rural areas.

Article 43A. *Participation of workers in management of industries*

The State shall take steps, by suitable legislation or in any other way, to secure the participation of workers in the management of undertakings, establishments or other organisations engaged in any industry.

Article 44. *Uniform civil code for the citizens*

The State shall endeavour to secure for the citizens a uniform civil code throughout the territory of India,

Article 45. *Provision for free and compulsory education for children*

The State shall endeavour to provide, within a period of ten years from the commencement of this Constitution, for free and compulsory education for all children until they complete the age of fourteen years.

Article 46. *Promotion of educational and economic interests of Scheduled Castes, Scheduled Tribes and other weaker sections*

The State shall promote with special care the educational and economic interests of the weaker sections of the people, and in particular, of the Scheduled Castes and the Scheduled Tribes, and shall protect them from social injustice and all forms of exploitation.

Article 47. *Duty of the State to raise the level of nutrition and the standard of living and to improve public health*

The State shall regard the raising of the raising of the level of nutrition and the standard of living of its people and the improvement of public health as among its primary duties and, in particular, the State shall endeavour to bring about prohibition of the consumption, except for medicinal purposes, of intoxicating drinks and of drugs which are injurious to health.

Article 48. *Organisation of agriculture and animal husbandry*

The State shall endeavour to organise agriculture and animal husbandry on modern and scientific lines and shall, in particular, takes steps for preserving and improving the breeds and prohibiting the slaughter of cows and calves and other milch and draught cattle.

Article 48A. *Protection and improvement of environment and safeguarding of forests and wild life*

The State shall endeavour to protect and improve the environment and to safeguard the forests and will life of the country.

Article 49. *Protection of monuments and places and objects of national importance*

It shall be the obligation of the State to protect every monument or place or object of artistic or historic interest, declared by or under law made by Parliament to be of national importance, from spoliation, disfigure-ment, destruction, removal, disposal or export, as the case may be.

Article 50. *Separation of judiciary from executive*

The State shall take steps to separate the judiciary from the executive in the public services of the State.

Article 51. *Promotion of international peace and security*

The State shall endeavour to.

(*a*) Promote international peace and security;

(*b*) Maintain just and honourable relations between nations;

(*c*) Foster respect for international law and treaty obligations in the dealings of organised people with one another; and

(*d*) Encourage settlement of international disputes by arbitration.

PART IV (A)
FUNDAMENTAL DUTIES

Article 51A. *Fundamental Duties*

It shall be the duty of every citizen of India-

(*a*) to abide by the Constitution and respect its ideals and institutions, the National Flag and the National Anthem:

(*b*) to cherish and follow the noble ideals which inspired our national struggle for freedom;

(*c*) to uphold and protect the sovereignty, unity and integrity of India;

(*d*) to defend the country and render national service when called upon to do so;
(*e*) to promote harmony and the spirit of common brotherhood amongst all the people of India transcending religious, linguistic and regional or sectional diversities; to renounce practices derogatory to the dignity of women;
(*f*) to value and preserve the rich heritage of our composite culture;
(*g*) to protect and improve the natural environment including forests, lakes, rivers, wild life and to have compassion for living creatures;
(*h*) to develop the scientific temper, humanism and the spirit of inquiry and reform;
(*i*) To safeguard public property and to abjure violence;
(*j*) to strive towards excellence in all spheres of individual and collective activity so that the nation constantly rises to higher levels of endeavour and achievement.

IMPLEMENTATION OF HUMAN RIGHTS IN INDIA

The implementation of Human Rights in India can be viewed under the following categories:

(*i*) Right to Education

Since Education develops human personality, understanding tolerance and comradeship, the right education is essential. Article 26 of UDHR and Article 13 of ICESCR recognises the right to education.

In India, there is no fundamental right to education. But its importance has been recognized in Article 41 of the Directive Principles of State Policy. It promises that State shall make effective efforts to secure to its citizens the right to education. The State is further obliged to endeavour to provide free and compulsory education to children up to the age of 14 years. While most of the states have introduced free primary education, it has not been possible to make it compulsory, perhaps due to financial compulsions.

There are concerted efforts however, to popularises adult education and make it purposeful, although, it is on a voluntary basis. Some states have provided free mid-day meals for students in primary Schools.

At the High School and University levels, State have strived to make education less expensive. Despite rapid increase in cost of living and continued hike in remunerations of academic and administrative staff, tution fees have remained static. Governments have also introduced concessions, and loan scholarships for deserving students. Members of Scheduled Castes and Tribes have, in many cases, been exempted from payment of regulars fees.

(*ii*) The Right to Life and Personal Liberty

Non-governmental organisations and the National and State Human Rights Commissions are being reported in the media a number of situation involving violation of the right to life and personal liberty at the instance of state agencies such as the security and police forces. Some of these situations are related to areas where there exist serious threats to internal security such as terrorism and insurgency and other are related to the law and order problems. A standing fact finding committee of the Legislative Council of Bihar (the first ever legislative committee appointed to investigate human rights violations in any state of India) is reported to have observed that human rights violations were common in the state and the "main targets have been the depressed and exploited classes, the dalits, women and children".

Many instances of custodial violence have been reported in the national media. They include violence by the police to human being during custody, rape and killing. A number of such instances have eventually reached the National Human Rights Commission, the High Courts and the Supreme Court.

The Indian army and paramilitary forces have often been pressed into services to meet the challenges of terrorism and insurgency, as the police force is not adequately equipped to meet such threats to civil life. While there are claims of rights violations by army and paramilitary forces. Some of which have been found proved by the National Human Rights Commission and the Indian Industry, the army claims that its human rights record has generally been exemplary.

Mindless acts of political expending by political parties, besides economic and other causes have contributed to terrorism in Punjab, Jammu and Kashmir. Instability in the North-East (Nagaland, Manipur, Tripura and Assam) has been the result of terrorism, insurgency and intertribal conflicts. Added to these is the politics – both natural as well as local – to shroud the real problem, i.e., economic backwardness. The borderline between a secessionist claim and a claim for autonomy is often determined by the political games which the parties to them play.

In a sense, the police have been largely an ill-equipped, under trained, overworked and under paid force. Their work has considerably expanded over time, but they are seriously handicapped for lack of resources. Apart from police reforms, a number of areas of criminal justice have been identified by the judiciary, the National Human Rights Commission (NHRC) and the Law Commission of India for reforms and to make the system of administration of criminal justice humane. The recent public outcry against some of the human rights violations by the security forces resulted in the termination of the Terrorist and Disruptive Activities (Prevention) Act, 1985-'91 (TADA), whereby the police and other security forces committed abuse of powers, and both the supreme court and the NHRC came down heavily on such abuses.

(*iii*) Right to Development

The ultimate objective of the whole Part IV of the Indian constitution requires the state to strive to promote the welfare of the people by securing and protecting as effectively as it may a social order in which social, economic and political justice shall inform all the institutions of the natural life.

The right to development in India in grossly impeded by the stupendous nature of the development problems which India faces. At the root of these problems are poverty, illiteracy and over population which form a vicious circle each contributing to the other. At the time of Independence, India's population was around 360 million. It is now about 1000 million. In 1970's, around 16 percent of the population was below the poverty line, now it has risen to 37 percent of the current population. These problems have a multiplier effect on all other social and economic problems.

There are parts of India, such as the tribal belts of the Districts of Kalahandi and Bolanjer in the state of Orissa, exposed to the scourge of poverty malnutrition and even starvation, attributed to repeated crop failures, in human exploitation of the tribal and politicisation of the human calamities.

The ninth five year plan (1997-2000) has a special thrust for rural development "with poverty alleviation programmer as its major component". The process of globalisation and liberalisation, now afoot in India has not found favour in certain quarters and the fear that it is harmful for the uplift of the poor is often expressed.

The International Labour Organisation, in its World Employment Report for 1996-'97, countered against economic liberalisation on all fronts at one go as it would lead to sharp increases in unemployment under-employment and poverty.

India has attained a discernible level of development for the last 50 years on many areas. It has mastered some of the most modern technologies such as those in the fields of communications, space and nuclear energy. But the magnitude of the problems engendered by poverty, illiteracy and popular explosive has affected negatively these achievements and demand more sustained efforts.

(*iv*) Right to Property

Right to property has become the most controversial right in the Indian society. There has been fair emphasis on the right to private property. It is said that it develops man's personality and is the fountain of all rights.

In India, there has been dual thinking on the concept of private property. In 1947, when India became independent, while the ruling congress party was in favour of land reforms; it was not against the institution of private property. It advocated land reforms because it wanted to stop exploitation of the tillers of land by absentee land holders. For this, while the Article 19 (1-f) of the Constitution guaranteed the right to acquire, hold and dispose of property if legalised the various land reforms as enacted by the state Governments by bringing in Article 31B,

The right to property is the fountain of all other rights. The freedom of expression and the press cannot be enjoyed without owing a press. Freedom of trade unions will be thwarted if they are not allowed to own property. Free movement throughout India would be meaningless if the people were to have no property or money and were not allowed to acquire property in places of their choice.

(v) Rights of Women

While violations of women's rights are not unknown in other societies, including the developed over, what aggravate them in the context of the Indian Society are poverty, illiteracy and some of the rationally and morally untenable social customs such as dowry, sati, etc.

The right to equality in the context of women has many aspects. A number of laws exists in the statute book related to the aspects of equal pay for equal work, equality of opportunity, equality before law, political equality of status and so on. But the implementation of these laws has left much to be desired.

The International movement for women's rights with the associated slogan that women's rights are human rights has gained momentum in the past decade. At the United Nations World Conference on Women in Nairobi (Kenya) in 1985, human rights began to emerge as a key issue for women, and by the 1995 World Conference on Women in Beijing (China) human rights became the frame work for the entire government plan of action.

Parliament enacted the Indecent Representation of Women (Prohibition) Act in 1986 to expand the law of obscenity contained in the Indian Penal Code, 1860 and to counter a growing tendency of indecent representation of or references to women in publications such as advertisements, which is derogatory of women. However, the implementation of this Act has not been effective.

Violence is described as a physical act or aggression of one individual or group against another or others. Violence against women means any act of violence which result in, or is likely to result in physical, sexual of psychological harm or suffering to women. There are the more latent and unquantifiable aspects of aggression or invasion of the self by outside agents namely emotional violence and other forms of cruelly which ends up in suicide, self-mutilation, negligence of ailments, sex determination tests and denial of food (Country report, 1995). In India, there has been a significant increase in reported crimes against women at least in certain metropolitan cities. A total of 232 cases of bride – burning were registered in Delhi between April 1983 and March 1984. In Delhi itself, there was one dowry death reported every 12 hours (Raina, 1984)

Apart from dowry-deaths or suicides, the incidents of wife-beating, cruelty, torture and humiliation were on the risk. This made the women's group demand that wife abuse and treated as on offence. The parliament responded with the criminal law (Second Amendment) Act, 1983, which for the first time gave legal recognition to domestic violence making 'cruelty', inflicted by the husband or his relatives on offence (Section, 498 A).

Parliament recently considered a law to reserve 33 percent of the seats in the Lok Sabha (the Lower House of Parliament) and the state legislative assemblies. This follows the 73rd constitution (Amendment) Act, 1986 which reserved 30 per cent of seats in councils at village, block and district levels. However, the male dominated political parties have so far stalled all attempts at getting the measure adopted into law.

In order to address the problems of implementation of women's rights, parliament enacted the National Commission of Women Act, 1990. Though the Act empowers the Commission to investigate, examine and review all matters relating to the safeguards provided for women under the constitution and other relevant laws, the commission feels that its powers are not equal to its tasks, and that it should have power to prosecute/summarily decide on cases of violation of gender justice.

Also, women's commissions are now functioning at the state level. Considering the traditional male domination in Indian society, these commission has a most unenviable task.

(*vi*) Right to Work

A person has been given the right to choose his profession under Article

19 (1-8) of the Indian Constitution. Article 39(a) which deals with Directive principles of state policy states that citizens have the right to an adequate means of livelihood.

The right to practice any profession is circumscribed by clause 6 of Article 19 which provides that the State may make laws relating to

(1) Professional and technical qualifications necessary for practising any profession or carrying on any occupation, trade or business.

(2) carrying on business partially or exclusively by State or, State controlled or managed corporations.

Restrictions on choice of profession are to control development of spurious professions. e.g., No person can practice medicine without being qualified in the study of medicine. Similarly no one can practice at the bar without having the appropriate qualification.

There is Article 24 of the Constitution which prohibits employment of children below the age of 14 years in a factory, mine or for hazardous work. There is also the Employment of children Act, 1938 which regulates employment of children workers in India have the right to join trade unions under Article 19 (1-c) of the Constitution. Besides they have the right to join trade unions of their choice under other relevant acts. The right, of protection against unemployment (Article 23 of UDHR) is unfortunately, is wanting in India although the State would wish to provide public assistance in case of unemployment under Article 41 of the Constitution.

This lack of right is consequential because there is no right to work. The right to work gives right to social security. It may be difficult for the State to secure work or social security for million of people.

The state of Maharashtra and Kerala has some sort of unemployment allowance Scheme on a limited Scale. The central and State Governments. are aware of the high rate of unemployment Unemployed graduates are encouraged to open their own business for which they are given necessary facilities.

(*vii*) Rights of the Child

All human rights must apply to the child also, as they are essential for the development of human rights. Two major aspects related to the rights of the child in Indian condition are:

(1) the violence against children and (2) the child labour.

The National crime records Bureau's report on "Crime in India" has reported a rise in crime against children in recent years. There are also reports of growing violence against street children in many urban areas. Parliament enacted the Justice Act, 1986 principally for the case, protection, treatment, development and rehabilitation of neglected or delinquent judgements.

The following new offences are created by it:

Cruelty to juvenile, employment of juvenile for begging, giving a juvenile intoxicating liquor or narcotic drug or psychotropic substances, and exploitation of juvenile employees.

It provides for juvenile homes for neglected children and special homes and observation homes for delinquent juveniles. But the number of such juvenile homes so far established been limited and those who exit are not properly run. Even a brutal murder of an inmate by another took place in Delhi observation home.

The most serious problem related to the rights of the child in India is the exploitation of children for a free or cheap labour. There is no reliable data work. But the estimate range from 20 million to 100 million. Usually children are engaged in a variety of industries or vocations such as, making of matches and fireworks, carpet making, glass bangle making, brass wares, plastic and rope weaving, salt extraction, making steel rolling and chips recycling, domestic work, prostitution, construction industry etc.

The painful reality of child labour exists despite the employment of children Act 1938 (Amendment 1985) child labour (Prohibition and regulation) Act, 1986 and other labour like the factories Act, 1948. Child labour exists more in unorganised sector than in organised which makes it detection difficult. Some of the non governmental organisa-tion are doing extremely effective work in this matter.

(*viii*) Rights of the Girl Child

The rights of the girl child have received a special emphasis the world over recently. India is notorious for its neglect of the girl child.

The deteriorating law and order situation compels one to lay certain physical limits on woman in the family, particularly the girls; quite unknowingly one has managed to control the freedom of a girl child though in all seriousness, it was merely intended to safeguarded her dignity.

There are instances when adults appear conscious of the rights of the girls because of conformity to world-wide efforts to bestow or ensure individuals their rights as acknowledged or accepted by democratic societies.

The problem of neglect of girl child is multifaceted, it encompasses foeticide, female illiteracy, social discrimination, child marriage and so on. There is a need for changing social attitudes through a process of social mobilisation. There is also a need for concerted administrative legal and social action to eliminate inequality of the girl child, female foeticide and female infanticides.

(*ix*) Right to Medical Care

Article 12 of the Covenant, ICESCR emphasizes on medical care of persons by the State. It assures physical, mental health and medical attention. Article 41 of the Constitution enjoins upon the State-to strive to give public assistance to sick and disabled persons. Within the limits of its economic capacity. Article 41 enjoins upon the State to raise the level of nutrition and improve public health.

States have tried to give medical aid by opening hospitals and other public health clinics, where free medical assistance is given to the people. Only a nominal fee is charged in some cases.

While medical attention is normally assured to people in the metropolitan cities of the country, the same type of medical attention and expertise is not available in towns and villages.

(*x*) Rights of Scheduled Castes and Scheduled Tribes

Majority of the scheduled castes and scheduled tribes are below the poverty line. The legal and political system provides for a range of measurer of affirmative discrimination in their favour, such as reservation of seats in legislation, reservation of jobs, reservation of seats in educational institutions, special scholarships etc. But much of them is yet suffer from inequality, and still subjected to indignities, humiliation and harassment by some of the members of more advanced classes in society.

The scheduled castes and scheduled tribes (prevention of atrocities) Act, 1989 has been introduced to stem the atrocities against them and to strengthen the constitutional interdiction. In 1990 the constitution was amended to establish a seven member high level National commission for SCs and STs to investigate and monitor all matters relating to the safeguard provided for SCs and STs, to examine specific complaints of violation of rights and safeguards, and to make recommendations to the government for effective implementation of these rights and safeguards.

The commission on scheduled castes and scheduled tribes has expressed concern over the rise in the number of atrocities, against SCs and STs protection of land rights has become a crucial issue. The economic backwardness of thee classes cannot be solved within the framework of reservation alone. The spread of education will help to remove the discrimination to a greater extent.

(*xi*) Rights of the Minorities

Although it is clear that the Indian context is different from the European, the term minority has not received adequate definition in the Indian context. Article 30 of the constitution speaks of "all minorities, whether based on religion or language". While it does not deny the existence of minorities identified on criteria other than religion or language, the current political vocabulary accepts only religious and linguistic minorities.

The partition of India into two countries resulted from the false apprehensive that the majority community in India would not ensure the rights of a minority community. The founding fathers of the constitution were indeed more keen to ensure the protection of religious minorities as part of the transition of India into independence. Yet India has had a tradition of tolerance and social synthesis of diverse religions, a tradition lately marred by the rise of groups and political parties advocating religious fanaticism. The politics of religion have to do with this more than anything else. Such groups were responsible for the pre-planned destruction of the Babri Masjid in December, 1992 which fomented considerable ill-feelings leading to several riots aimed more at one community than the other (Mani, 1998).

The National Commission for Minorities Act was enacted in 1992 aimed protection of religious minorities such as Muslims, Sikhs, Buddhists and Parsis. Spread of secular education should go a long way in providing a firm foundation for development of minorities in India.

(*xii*)Violation of Human Rights

Considering the present scenario in the country, one finds that despite extensive Constitutional and statutory safeguards, serious human rights abuses are taking place. This is evident from the number of complaints of human rights violation which are received by the National and State Human Rights Commissions. These violations include the following:

(*i*) Child labour.

(*ii*) Bonded labour, sale of children.

(*iii*) Rape of women in police custody

(iv) Torture and death of suspected culprits in police custody
(v) Trial delays
(vi) Extra-judicial execution of suspected militants by security forces.
(vii) Killing of suspected militants in fake encounters
(viii) Female infanticide
(ix) Extortion, ethnic killings and foeticide, political slayings and
(x) Kidnapping for ransom.

AGENCIES PROMOTED HUMAN RIGHTS IMPLEMENTATION IN INDIA

The responsibility for implementation of human rights falls on the state and its legislative and executive machinery. The state has the duty to protect and promote individual and group rights. When we examine the Indian condition after the emergency period, we can see four catalytic agencies which promote human rights implementation. They are the following:

1. The Judiciary
2. NGOs
3. The Media
4. National Human Rights Commission

The Judiciary

Judiciary performs the function of implementation of human rights mainly by innovative interpretation and assumption of its jurisdiction and by innovative interpretation and application of the human rights provisions of the constitution. The Supreme Court of India has declared that it has a special responsibility to enlarge the range and meaning of the fundamental rights and advance of the human rights jurisprudence.

The major two contributions of judiciary to the human rights jurisprudence are the following:

(1) Substantive expansion of the concept of human rights under Article 21 of the Constitution.

(2) The procedural innovation of public interest litigation

The Supreme Court of India and the State High Courts have broad powers under the constitution in respect of enforcement of fundamental rights and that they have liberally interpreted these powers.

The role of NGOs and NHRC are described in detail.

Non Governmental Organisations (NGOs)

NGOs, both national as well or international are performing useful work in the monitoring and implementation of human rights.

The Nature and Characteristics of NGOs

From the outset, it is essential to recognize that the human rights movement is comprised of two broad categories of NGOs.

The first is the "ideal" or "exclusive" human NGO whose *raison d' etre* derives from the fight for human rights. This includes international NGOs like Amnesty International, regional bodies such as Caribbean Human Rights, national bodies like the people's Union for Civil Liberties in India or the Uganda Human Rights Activists, and local organisations such as the Alberta Human Rights and Civil Liberties Association Canada.

The "ideal" human NGO is a voluntary organisation which is independent of both government and all groups which seek direct political power, and which does not itself seek such power. Typically, too, the human rights NGO monitors government behaviour and tries to hold the government accountable to human rights standards of human rights embodies in either international instruments or national legislation.

The legitimacy and credibility of a human rights organisation rests is large part on the objectivity of its fact-finding and the integrity with which it applies international human rights standards. A group which allies itself with government or opposition, seeks political power and office for itself, or subordinates human rights concerns to other political objectives, no matter how noble, has moved beyond the compass of human rights work.

Far more numerous than these exclusive human rights NGOs are NGOs which have broader or different primary goals but which devote substantial resources to the human rights struggle. This category includes churches; trade unions; peasant organisations; women's organisations, professional associations (of lawyers, journalists, doctors, educators, scientists); ethnically-based associations;

indigenous peoples' organisations; groups concerned with children, refugees, the elderly, handicapped persons, the poor, or consumers; NGOs focused on development or the environment; and that broad class of organisations referred to as peoples' organisations.

In some instances, such NGOs have established special human rights committees to spearhead their human rights activities; others have simply written human rights planks into larger platforms or programmes. Often, such organisations did not begin with a specific human rights agendas but came rapidly to activities involving the promotion and protection of human rights. In other instances, individuals determined to engage in human rights action, but blocked by governmental regulations from registering as a human rights NGO, carry out human rights work under the guise of a social or cultural association, a consumer group, or a development organisation.

Any one of these groups may be an important actor in the human rights arena and all contribute in a fundamental way to the political pluralism that is the basis of the democratic political process. Any of these groups may become a significant ally for a human rights organisation in a particular battle. What distinguishes a human rights NGO from other political actors is that the latter, typically, seek to protect the right of their members ore constituents only; a human rights groups seeks to secure the rights for all members of the society. A political group seeks to advance its own particular interests or programmes; a human rights group seeks to keep the political process open to all legitimate societal forces.

Functions of NGOs

The following are the functions of NGOs:

(i) Information Gathering, Evaluation and Dissemination: One of the most important functions performed by NGOs engaged in human rights work is that of monitoring the behaviour of the state and of other power elites-of gathering, evaluating and disseminating information and, in the process, exposing human rights violations.

This is a vital function because, unless their behaviour is monitored, governments will not be held accountable. The importance of information emerges in part from the paradox that is central to the human rights struggle; that the main protector of human rights(the authority one must in the end rely on to enforce human rights standards) is also the main violator. While information is not sufficient to halt human rights abuses, it is a precondition for stopping abuses and a prerequisite for effective action in the human rights field.

NGOs provide information to their own constituencies, their governments and the mass media. They also provide information to inter-governmental organisations charged with human rights responsibilities.

The information or fact-finding function of NGOs has come under serious scrutiny, especially from governments charged with committing violations and from their supporters. As a consequence, many in the human rights community have been sensitised to the need for their data to pass tests of validity (particularly as to source of the information-e.g,., how credible are the witnesses) and reliability (quantity and quality).

With respect to information, it is important to recognize that NGOs are often in a better position than government agencies both to collect and to assess information with respect to the observance of economic, social and cultural rights at the grassroots. They frequently have access to, and the trust of, those at the base of society, whether in the urban or rural sectors, and especially among the marginalized. While fact-finding with respect to economic, social and cultural rights is an area that has been largely neglected by international human rights NGOs, it is an area of prime concern to local and national NGOs, especially in the Third World.

(ii) Advocacy to Stop Abuses and Secure Redress: "Advocacy", as a legal term, means pleading on behalf of someone else. The counterpart to advocacy in religious terminology is "witnessing". Whether used in the legal or religious sense, advocacy is initially dependent on information processing yet goes beyond that function. It means actively taking up the case of those whose rights are violated.

For a human rights organisation, advocacy may mean speaking out for the voiceless and, in this fashion, it entails expanding and making more visible what may be only a latent conflict. Frequently advocacy involves challenging orthodox interpretations and, at times, it involves breaking completely new ground, focusing public attention on an issue that has been totally ignored and outside the public consciousness.

(iii) Legal Aid, Scientific Expertise and Humanitarian Assistance : Legal aid refers to a range of law-related activities-engagement of legal defence, provision of co-counsel, filing writs of *habeas corpus*, filing *amicus curiae* briefs, sending legally-trained foreign-national observers to public trials, up to and including publication of "political show trials" so carefully staged by repressive regimes-on behalf of individuals or organisations accused of such vague political crimes as "conspiracy", "subversion" and "slander of the State".

In recent years, another type of related expert assistance has been provided to victims by NGOs i.e., expertise which derives from the scientific community, Thus, forensic scientists have helped in identifying bodies buried in mass graves or in performing autopsies on people who have died in police custody or under suspicious circumstances, and lawyers and forensic scientists have collaborated to develop standards for conducting such autopsies. Geneticists have helped in matching "disappeared" Argentine children with their grandparents and have established a gene bank for this purpose. More generally, physicians and other health workers have provided treatment to torture victims; they have investigated the medical consequences of the use of tear gas and plastic bullets; and they have conducted research into the health impact of disasters such as Bhopal and Chernoby1.

***(iv) Lobbying National and International Authorities*:** Lobbying is the process through which interests are articulated and aggregated. Lobbying may also be directed at co-interest groups to mobilize their support; and it may involve the pressuring of corporations, banks, international financial institutions and inter-governmental organisations.

Within the international organisational context, NGOs will lobby expert members of key human rights bodies, or governments, or officials of the organisation in order to get the votes necessary to pass a resolution, have an item inscribed into the agenda, establish a rapporteur, or commit the organisation to a pro-human rights course of action.

Predisposed to utilize democratic tactics and strategies, many national NGOs concerned with human rights have become as professional as other private interest groups in lobbying within their own country. Some have also learned how to take their case to international arenas and forums when domestic remedies are exhausted; e.g., to the UN Human Rights Committee, the UN

Commission on Human Rights, its Sub-Commission, or the Sub-Commission's working Groups on Indigenous Populations or on slavery.

(v) Legislation to Incorporate or Develop Human Rights Standards : NGOs recognize that law on the books is not law in fact-that law must be implemented, not merely drafted-nonetheless, substantial efforts have been devoted to bringing national legislation into conformity with international human rights standards. Thus, NGOs are often engaged in drafting legislative proposals, preparing position papers on pending legislation, and testifying before parliamentary or other government committees. This has been particularly true in periods of transition from authoritarian or military regimes to democratic ones.

(vi) Education, Conscientization of Empowerment : NGOs have come to realize that people cannot defend their rights unless they know their rights. Only through education and conscientization can NGOs combat the status quo in which large groups at the base of society are effectively excluded from political participation in decisions so fundamentally affecting their lives, including resource allocation, the choice of technology, and the development model.

The educational efforts that engage NGOs in the human rights area tend to be at the non-formal level, rather than the formal school setting, and involve consultations, workshops and seminars, and training courses for women, trade unionists, peasants, the indigenous or church people. New methodologies have been developed, especially for teaching the illiterate, including street theatre, comic books, poster competitions, folk music, films, videos and games. The educational efforts have also been heavily directed towards developing self-reliance, as with participatory research, skills development and leadership training.

(vii) Building Solidarity : Even though human rights struggles are fought and won largely in national arenas-by organizing and mobilizing in the slums and *the barrios*, by conscientizing people about their rights and how to fight for them-the role of international support cannot be underestimated.

Building solidarity across different sectors of society-between workers and peasants, women's organisations, organisations of indigenous peoples-and across ethnic and religious groups, is a task taken on by many organisations working in the human rights arena. Particularly in large or heterogenous societies, many NGOs recognize that change will come only by a radical restructuring of the social order; and for such a restructuring, lines of solidarity must be built across communities that have been fragmented, isolated and marginalized, and often mobilized communally against each other. Hence, efforts are directed towards information sharing and networking as a first step towards such creating such solidarity and overcoming an "apartheid" mentality.

(viii) Delivery of Services **:** This function is rather different from the others. It involves less protection from state power and more helping, often in collaboration with the state, to realize economic, social and cultural rights, and sometimes civil and political ones.

In the last two decades, many governments have come to realize that NGOs are better able to deliver service than government authorities. This may pertain to such things as reaching victims in disaster relief, assistance to refugee populations, providing skills training for underprivileged groups, offering course in human rights education to military and police, offering legal aid to those who cannot afford it. In these cases, governments have tried to co opt NGOs into becoming instruments for delivering services then should be providing, but are unable to provide.

(ix) Keeping Open the Political System : Human rights NGOs are not mass based organisations. They work with, but are generally different from, "people's organisations".

The human rights organisation is different because its purpose is largely to keep the political process open and to keep the government accountable so that power is not inordinately centralized or abused. It is for this reason that killing human rights monitors or preventing human rights groups from operating, is particularly devastating because, by those acts, one directly undermines all other independent societal forces.

There are a number of NGOs, both national as well as international, performing useful work in the monitoring and implementation of human rights. Indeed, there are NGOs with political or other motives and those wedded to selfless service.

Among the foreign or 'international' NGOs, the Amnesty International (AI), the Human Rights Watch/Asia (HRWA) and the

International Commission of Jurists (ICJ) are prominent in the field of civil and political rights. AI was highly rated in India for its reports on human rights violations in India during the emergency (1975-77).

A brief description of Amnesty International is given below:

(i) AMNESTY INTERNATIONAL

Amnesty International forms a global community of human rights defenders with the principles of international solidarity, effective action for the individual victim, global coverage, the universality and indivisibility of human rights, impartiality and independence, and democracy and mutual respect.

Vision and Mission: Amnesty International's vision is of a world in which every person enjoys all of the human rights enshrined in the Universal Declaration of Human Rights and other international human rights standards.

In pursuit of this vision, Amnesty International's mission is to undertake research and action focused on preventing and ending grave abuses of the rights to physical and mental integrity, freedom of conscience and expression, and freedom from discrimination, within the context of its work to promote all human rights.

Procedure: Amnesty International addresses governments, intergovernmental organizations, armed political groups, companies and other non-state actors. AI seeks to disclose human rights abuses accurately, quickly and persistently. It systematically and impartially researches the facts of individual cases and patterns of human rights abuses. These findings are publicized, and members, supporters and staff mobilize public pressure on governments and others to stop the abuses.

In addition to its work on specific abuses of human rights, Amnesty International urges all governments to observe the rule of law, and to ratify and implement human rights standards; it carries out a wide range of human rights educational activities; and it encourages intergovernmental organizations, individuals, and all organs of society to support and respect human rights.

Ultimate authority for the conduct of the affairs of AI is vested in the International Council. The International Council establish systems and bodies of governance and delegation for the movement, elect members to those bodies, and hold those bodies and their members accountable.

Executive Committee: There is an International Executive Committee. The primary role of the International Executive Committee is to provide leadership and stewardship for the whole of Amnesty International worldwide. The major functions of the International Executive Committee are:

(*i*) to take international decisions on behalf of AI
(*ii*) to ensure that there is a sound financial policy for AI and that the financial policy is consistently implemented across the international organization
(*iii*) to ensure implementation of the Integrated Strategic Plan;
(*iv*) to hold sections, structures and other bodies of A I accountable for their functioning by presenting reports to the International Council;
(*v*) to perform the other functions conferred on it by the Statute.

The day-to-day affairs of AI shall be conducted by the International Secretariat headed by a Secretary General under the direction of the International Executive Committee.

Responsibility for A I work on abuses of human rights in any country or territory, including the collection and evaluation of information, and the sending of delegations, lies with the international governing bodies of the organization, and not with the section, groups or members in the country or territory concerned.

A section of AI may be established in any country, state, territory or region with the consent of the International Executive Committee. Groups of not less than five members may, on payment of an annual fee determined by the International Council, become affiliated to AI or a section thereof. Any dispute as to whether a group should be or remain affiliated shall be decided by the International Executive Committee.

Individuals residing in countries, states, territories or regions where there is no section may, on payment to the International Secretariat of an annual subscription fee determined by the International Executive Committee, become members of AI with the consent of the International Executive Committee. In countries where a section exists, individuals may become international members of AI with the consent of the section and of the International Executive

Committee. The International Secretariat shall maintain a register of such members.

Membership of or affiliation to AI may be terminated at any time by resignation in writing.

Finance: An auditor appointed by the International Council shall annually audit the accounts of AI which shall be prepared by the International Secretariat and presented to the International Executive Committee and the International Council.

No part of the income or property of AI shall directly or indirectly be paid or transferred otherwise than for valuable and sufficient consideration to any of its members by way of dividend, gift, division, bonus or otherwise howsoever by way of profit.

NATIONAL HUMAN RIGHTS COMMISSION (NHRC)

Details of the working of the NHRC constituted on 28th Sept. 1993, as per The Protection of Human Rights Act, are given below.

The Protection of Human Rights Act, 1993 is an Act to provide for the constitution of a National Human Rights Commission, State Human Rights Commission in States and Human Rights Courts for better protection of Human Rights and for matters connected therewith or incidental thereto.

Some of the basic ideas related to the Protection of Human Rights Act are listed here.

Short title, extent and commencement

(*i*) This Act may be called the Protection of Human Rights Act, 1993.

(*ii*) It extends to the whole of India.

Provided that it shall apply to the State of Jammu and Kashmir only in so far as it pertains to the matters relatable to any of the entries enumerated in List I or List lll in the Seventh Schedule to the Constitution as applicable to that State.

(*iii*) It shall be deemed to have come into force on the 28th day of September, 1993.

Definitions

(1) In this Act, unless the context otherwise requires-

(*a*) "armed forces" means the naval, military and air forces and includes any other armed forces of the Union;

(*b*) "Chairperson" means the Chairperson of the Commission or of the State Commission, as the case may be;

(*c*) "Commission" means the National Human Rights Commission

(*d*) "human rights" means the rights relating to life, liberty, equality and dignity of the individual guaranteed by the Constitution or embodied in the International Covenants and enforceable by courts in India.

(*e*) "Human Rights Court" means the Human Rights Court specified under section 30;

(*f*) "Member" means a Member of the Commission or of the State Commission, as the case may be, and includes the Chairperson;

(*g*) "Public servant" shall have the meaning assigned to it in section 21 of the Indian Penal Code;

(*h*) "State Commission" means a State Human Rights Commission constituted under section 21.

(2) Any reference in this Act to a law, which is not in force in the State of Jammu and Kashmir, shall, in relation to that State, be construed as a reference to a corresponding law, if any, in force in that State.

Constitution

According to the Protection of human Rights Act,

(1) The Central Government shall constitute a body to be known as the National Human Rights Commission to exercise the powers conferred upon, and to perform the functions assigned to it, under this Act.

(2) The Commission shall consist of

(*a*) A Chairperson who has been a Chief Justice of the Supreme Court;

(*b*) One Member who is or has been, a Judge of the Supreme Court;

(*c*) One Member who is, or has been, the Chief Justice of a High Court;

(*d*) Two Members to be appointed from amongst persons having knowledge of, or practical experience in, matters relating to human rights.

(3) The Chairpersons of the National Commission for Minorities, the National Commission for the Scheduled Castes and Scheduled Tribes and the National Commission for Women shall be deemed to be Members of the Commission for the discharge of functions specified in clauses (*b*) to (j) of section 12.

(4) There shall be a Secretary-General who shall be the Chief Executive Officer of the Commission and shall exercise such powers and discharge such functions of the Commission as it may delegate to him.

(5) The headquarters of the Commission shall be at Delhi and the Commission may, with the previous approval of the Central Government, establish offices at other places in India.

Appointment of Chairperson and other Members

(1) The Chairperson and other Members shall be appointed by the President by warrant under his hand and seal. Provided that every appointment under this sub-section shall be made after obtaining the recommendations of a Committee consisting of

(*a*) The Prime Minister —Chairperson

(*b*) Speaker of the House of the People — Member

(*c*) Minister in-charge of the Ministry of Home Affairs in the Government of India — Member

(*d*) Leader of the Opposition in the House of the People — Member

(*e*) Leader of the Opposition in the Council of States — Member

(*f*) Deputy Chairman of the Council of States — Member

Provided further that no sitting Judge of the Supreme Court or sitting Chief Justice of a High Court shall be appointed except after consultation with the Chief Justice of India.

(2) No appointment of a Chairperson or a Member shall be invalid merely by reason of any vacancy in the Committee.

Removal of a Member of the Commission

(1) Subject to the provisions of sub-section (2), the Chairperson or any other Member of the Commission shall only be removed from his office by order of the President on the ground of proved or incapacity after the Supreme Court, on reference being made to it by the President, has, on inquiry held in accordance with the procedure prescribed in that behalf by the Supreme Court, reported that the Chairperson or such other Member, as the case may be, ought on any such ground to be removed.

(2) Notwithstanding anything in sub-section (1), the President may by order remove from office the Chairperson or any other Member if the Chairperson or such other Member, as the case may be

(*a*) is adjudged an insolvent; or

(*b*) engages during his term of office in any paid employment out side the duties of his office: or

(*c*) is unfit to continue in office by reason of infirmity of mind or body; or

(*d*) is of unsound mind and stands so declared by a competent court; or

(*e*) is convicted and sentenced to imprisonment for an offence which in the opinion of the President involves moral turpitude.

Term of Office of Members

(1) A person appointed as Chairperson shall hold office for a term of five years from the date on which he enters upon his office or until he attains the age of seventy years, whichever is earlier.

(2) A person appointed as a Member shall hold office for a term of five years from the date on which he enters upon his office and shall be eligible for re-appointment for another term of five years. Provided that no Member shall hold office after he has attained the age of seventy years.

(3) On ceasing to hold office, a Chairperson or a Member shall be ineligible for further employment under the Government of India or under the Government of any State.

Member to act as Chairperson or to discharge his functions in certain circumstances

(1) In the event of the occurrence of any vacancy in the office of the Chairperson by reason of his death, resignation or otherwise, the President may, by notification, authorise one of the Members to act as the Chairperson until the appointment of a new Chairperson to fill such vacancy.

(2) When the Chairperson is unable to discharge his functions owing to absence on leave or otherwise, such one of the Members as the President may, by notification, authorise in this behalf, shall discharge the functions of the Chairperson until the date on which the Chairperson resumes his duties.

Terms and Conditions of Service of Members

The salaries and allowances payable to, and other terms and conditions of service of, the Members shall be such as may be prescribed. Provided that neither the salary and allowances nor the other terms and conditions of service of a Member shall be varied to his disadvantage after his appointment.

Vacancies, etc., not to invalidate the proceedings of the Commission.

No act or proceedings of the Commission shall be questioned or shall be invalidated merely on the ground of existence of any vacancy or defect in the constitution of the Commission.

Procedure to be Regulated by the Commission

(1) The Commission shall meet at such time and place as the Chairperson may think fit.

(2) The Commission shall regulate its own procedure.

(3) All orders and decisions of the Commission shall be audited by the Secretary-General or any other officer of the Commission duly authorised by the Chairperson in this behalf.

Officers and other staff of the Commission

(1) The Central Government shall make available to the Commission:

(*a*) an officer of the rank of the Secretary to the Government of India who shall be the Secretary-General of the Commission; and (b) such police and investigative staff under an officer not below the rank of a Director General of Police and such other officers and staff as may be necessary for the efficient performance of the functions of the Commission.

(2) Subject to such rules as may be made by the Central Government in this behalf, the Commission may appoint such other administrative, technical and scientific staff as it may consider necessary.

(3) The salaries, allowances and conditions of service of the officers and other staff appointed under sub-section (2) shall be such as may be prescribed.

Functions and Powers of the Commission

Functions of the Commission

The Commission shall perform all or any of the following functions, namely:

(*a*) inquire, sue mote or on a petition presented to it by a victim or any person on his behalf, into complaint of (*i*) violation of human rights or abetment thereof or

(*ii*) negligence in the prevention of such violation, by a public servant;

(*b*) intervene in any proceeding involving any allegation of violation of human rights pending before a court with the approval of such court;

(*c*) visit, under intimation to the State Government, any jail or any other institution under the control of the State Government, where persons are detained or lodged for purposes of treatment, reformation or protection to study the living conditions of the inmates and make recommendations thereon;

(*d*) review the safeguards provided by or under the Constitution or any law for the time being in force for the protection of human rights and recommend measures for their effective implementation;

(*e*) review the factors, including acts of terrorism that inhibit the enjoyment of human rights and recommend appropriate remedial measures;

(*f*) study treaties and other international instruments on human rights and make recommendations for their effective implementation;

(*g*) undertake and promote research in the field of human rights;

(*h*) spread human rights literacy among various sections of society and promote awareness of the safeguards available for the protection of these rights through publications, the media, seminars and other available means;

(*i*) encourage the efforts of non-governmental organisations and institutions working in the field of human rights;

(*j*) such other functions as it may consider necessary for the protection of human rights.

Powers Relating to Inquiries

(1) The Commission shall, while inquiring into complaints under this Act, have all the powers of a civil court trying a suit under the Code of Civil Procedure, 1908, and in particular in respect of the following matters, namely:

(*a*) summoning and enforcing the attendance of witnesses and examining them on oath;
(*b*) discovery and production of any document;
(*c*) receiving evidence on affidavits;

(*d*) requisitioning any public record or copy thereof from any court or office;

(*e*) issuing commissions for the examination of witnesses or documents;

(*f*) any other matter which may be prescribed.

(2) The Commission shall have power to require any person, subject to any privilege which may be claimed by that person under any law for the time being in force, to furnish information on such points or matters as, in the opinion of the Commission, may be useful for, or relevant to, the subject matter of the inquiry and any person so required shall be deemed to be legally bound to furnish such information within the meaning of section 176 and section 177 of the Indian Penal Code.

(3) The Commission or any other officer, not below the rank of a Gazetted Officer, specially authorised in this behalf by the Commission may enter any building or place where the Commission has reason to believe that any document relating to the subject matter of the inquiry may be found, and may seize any such document or take extracts or copies there from subject to the provisions of section 100 of the Code of Criminal Procedure, 1973, in so far as it may be applicable.

(4) The Commission shall be deemed to be a civil court and when any offence as is described in section 175, section 178, section 179, section 180 or section 228 of the Indian Penal Code is committed in the view or presence of the Commission, the Commission may, after recording the facts constituting the offence and the statement of the accused as provided for in the Code of Criminal Procedure, 1973, forward the case to a Magistrate having jurisdiction to try the same and the Magistrate to whom any such case is forwarded shall proceed to hear the complaint against the accused as if the case has been forwarded to him under section 346 of the Code of Criminal Procedure, 1973.

(5) Every proceeding before the Commission shall be deemed to be a judicial proceeding within the meaning of sections 193 and 228, and for the purposes of section 196, of the Indian Penal Code, and the Commission shall be deemed to be a civil court for all the purposes of section 195 and Chapter XXVI of the Code of Criminal Procedure, 1973.

Investigation

(1) The Commission may, for the purpose of conducting any investigation pertaining to the inquiry, utilise the services of any officer or investigation agency of the Central Government or any State Government with the concurrence of the Central Government or the State Government, as the case may be.

(2) For the purpose of investigating into any matter pertaining to the inquiry, any officer or agency whose services are utilised under sub-section (1) may, subject to the direction and control of the Commission.

(*a*) summon and enforce the attendance of any person and examine him;

(*b*) require the discovery and production of any document; and

(*c*) requisition any public record or copy thereof from any office.

(3) The provisions of section 15 shall apply in relation to any statement made by a person before any officer or agency whose services are utilised under sub-section (1) as they apply in relation to any statement made by a person in the course of giving evidence before the Commission.

(4) The officer or agency whose services are utilised under sub-section (1) shall investigate into any matter pertaining to the inquiry and submit a report thereon to the Commission within such period as may be specified by the Commission in this behalf

(5) The Commission shall satisfy itself about the correctness of the facts stated and the conclusion, if any, arrived at in the report subjected to it under sub-section (4) and for this purpose the Commission may make such inquiry (including the examination of the person or persons who conducted or assisted in the investigation) as it thinks fit.

Statement Made by Persons to the Commission

No statement made by a person in the course of giving evidence before the Commission shall subject him to, or be used against him in, any civil or criminal proceeding except a prosecution for giving false evidence by such statement: Provided that the statement—

(*a*) is made in reply to the question which he is required by the Commission to answer; or

(*b*) is relevant to the subject matter of the inquiry.

Persons Likely to be Prejudicially Affected to be Heard

If, at any stage of the inquiry, the Commission—

(*a*) considers it necessary to inquire into the conduct of any person; or

(*b*) is of the opinion that the reputation of any person is likely to be prejudicially affected by the inquiry;it shall give to that person a reasonable opportunity of being heard in the inquiry and to produce evidence in his defence: Provided that nothing in this section shall apply where the credit of a witness is being impeached.

Procedure

Inquiry into complaints: The Commission while inquiring into the complaints of violations of human rights may—

(*i*) call for information or report from the Central Government or any State Government or any other authority or organisation subordinate thereto within such time as may be specified by it;

Provided that—

(*a*) if the information or report is not received within the time stipulated by the Commission, it may proceed to inquire re into the complaint on its own;

(*b*) if, on receipt of information or report, the Commission is satisfied either that no further inquiry is required or that the required action has been initiated or taken by the concerned Government or authority, it may not proceed with the complaint and inform the complainant accordingly,

(*ii*) without prejudice to anything contained in clause (*i*), if it confers necessary, having regard to the nature of the complaint, initiate an inquiry.

Steps after Inquiry: The Commission may take any of the following steps upon the completion of an inquiry held under this Act namely :

(1) where the inquiry discloses, the commission of violation of human rights or negligence in the prevention of violation of human

rights by a public servant, it may recommend to the concerned Government or authority the initiation of proceedings for prosecution or such other action as the Commission may deem fit against the concerned person or persons;

(2) approach the Supreme Court or the High Court concerned for such directions, orders or writs as that Court may deem necessary;

(3) recommend to the concerned Government or authority for the grant of such immediate interim relief to the victim or the members of his family as the Commission may consider necessary;

(4) subject to the provisions of clause (5), provide a copy of the inquiry report to the petitioner or his representative;

(5) the Commission shall send a copy of its inquiry report together with its recommendations to the concerned Government or authority and the concerned Government or authority shall, within a period of one month, or such further time as the Commission may allow, forward its comments on the report, including the action taken or proposed to be taken thereon, to the Commission;

(6) the Commission shall publish its inquiry report together with the comments of the concerned Government or authority, if any, and the action taken or proposed to be taken by the concerned Government or authority on the recommendations of the Commission.

Procedure with Respect to Armed Forces

(1) Notwithstanding anything contained in this Act, while dealing with complaints of violation of human rights by members of the armed forces, the Commission shall adopt the following procedure, namely:

(*a*) it may, either on its own motion or on receipt of a petition, seek a report from the Central Government;

(*b*) after the receipt of the report, it may, either not proceed with the complaint or, as the case may be, make its recommenda-tions to that Government.

(2) The Central Government shall inform the Commission of the action taken on the recommendations within three months or such further time as the Commission may allow.

(3) The Commission shall publish its report together with its recommendations made to the Central Government and the action taken by that Government on such recommendations.

(4) The Commission shall provide a copy of the report published under sub-section (3) to the petitioner or his representative.

Annual and Special Reports of the Commission

(1) The Commission shall submit an annual report to the Central Government and to the State Government concerned and may at any time submit special reports on any matter which, in its opinion, is of such urgency or importance that it should not be deferred till submission of the annual report.

(2) The Central Government and the State Government, as the case may be, shall cause the annual and special reports of the Commission to be laid before each House of Parliament or the State Legislature respectively, as the case may be, along with a memorandum of action taken or proposed to be taken on the recommendations of the Commission and the reasons for non-acceptance of the recommendations, if any.

STATE HUMAN RIGHTS COMMISSIONS

Constitution of State Human Rights Commissions

As per the Protection of Human Rights Act,

(1) A State Government may constitute a body to be known as the ... (name of the State) Human Rights Commission to exercise the powers conferred upon, and to perform the functions assigned to, a State Commission under this chapter.

(2) The State Commission shall consist of

- (*a*) a Chairperson who has been a Chief Justice of a High Court;
- (*b*) one Member who is, or has been, a Judge of a High Court;
- (*c*) one Member who is, or has been, a district judge in that State;
- (*d*) two Members to be appointed from amongst persons having knowledge of, or practical experience in, matters relating to human rights.

(3) There shall be a Secretary who shall be the Chief Executive Officer of the State Commission and shall exercise such powers and dis-charge such functions of the State Commission as it may delegate to him.

(4) The headquarters of the State Commission shall be at such place as the State Government may, by notification, specify.

(5) A State Commission may inquire into violation of human rights only in respect of matters relatable to any of the entries enumerated in List II and List lll in the Seventh Schedule to the Constitution:

Provided that if any such matter is already being inquired into by the Commission or any other Commission duly constituted under any law for the time being in force, the State Commission shall not inquire into the said matter:Provided further that in relation to the Jammu and Kashmir Human Rights Commission, this sub-section shall have effect as if for the words and figures "List ll and List lll in the Seventh Schedule to the Constitution", the words and figures "List lll in the Seventh Schedule to the Constitution as applicable to the State of Jammu and Kashmir and in respect of matters in relation to which the Legislature of that State has power to make laws" had been substituted.

Appointment of Chairperson and other Members of State Commission

(1) The Chairperson and other Members shall be appointed by the Governor by warrant under his hand and seal:

Provided that every appointment under this sub-section shall be made after obtaining the recommendation of a Committee consisting of

(*a*) the Chief Minister — Chairperson

(*b*) Speaker of the Legislative — Member Assembly

(*c*) Minister in-charge of the Department — Member of Home, in that State

(*d*) Leader of the Opposition in the — Member Legislative Assembly

Provided further that where there is a Legislative Council in a State, the Chairman of that Council and the Leader of the Opposition in that Council shall also be members of the Committee.

Provided also that no sitting Judge of a High Court or a sitting District Judge shall be appointed except after consultation with the Chief Justice of the High Court of the concerned State

(2) No appointment of a Chairperson or a Member of the State Commission shall be invalid merely by reason of any vacancy in the Committee.

Removal of a Member of the State Commission

(1) Subject to the provisions of sub-section (2), the Chairperson or any other member of the State Commission shall only be removed from his office by order of the President on the ground of proved misbehaviour or incapacity after the Supreme Court, on a reference being made to it by the President, has, on inquiry held in accordance with the procedure prescribed in that behalf by the Supreme Court, reported that the Chairperson or such other Member, as the case may be, ought on any such ground to be removed.

(2) Notwithstanding anything in sub-section (1), the President may by order remove from office the Chairperson or any other Member if the Chairperson or such other Member, as the case may be–

(*a*) is adjudged an insolvent; OR

(*b*) engages during his term of office in any paid employment outside the duties of his office; OR

(*c*) is unfit to continue in office by reason of infirmity of mind or body; OR

(*d*) is of unsound mind and stands so declared by a competent court; OR

(*e*) is convicted and sentenced to imprisonment for an offence which in the opinion of the President involves moral turpitude.

Term of office of Members of the State Commission

(1) A person appointed as Chairperson shall hold office for a term of five years from the date on which he enters upon his office or until he attains the age of seventy years, whichever is earlier;

(2) A person appointed as a Member shall hold office for a term of five years from the date on which he enters upon his office and shall be eligible for re-appointment for another term of five years;Provided that no Member shall hold office after he has attained the age of seventy years

(3) On ceasing to hold office, a Chairperson or a Member shall be ineligible for further employment under the Government of a State or under the Government of India.

Member to act as Chairperson or to discharge his functions in certain circumstances

(1) In the event of the occurrence of any vacancy in the office of the Chairperson by reason of his death, resignation or otherwise, the Governor may, by notification, authorise one of the Members to act as the Chairperson until the appointment of a new Chairperson to fill such vacancy.

(2) When the Chairperson is unable to discharge his functions owing to absence on leave or otherwise, such one of the Members as the Governor may, by notification, authorise in this behalf, shall discharge the functions of the Chairperson until the date on which the Chairperson resumes his duties.

Terms and Conditions of Service of Members of the State Commission

The salaries and allowances payable to, and other terms and conditions of service of, the Members shall be such as may be prescribed by the State Government.

Provided that neither the salary and allowances nor the other terms and conditions of service of a Member shall be varied to his disadvantage after his appointment.

Officers and Other Staff of the State Commission

(1) The State Government shall make available to the Commission

(*a*) an officer not below the rank of a Secretary to the State Government who shall be the Secretary of the State Commission; and

(*b*) such police and investigative staff under an officer not below the rank of an Inspector General of Police and such other officers and staff as may be necessary for the efficient performance of the functions of the State Commission

(2) subject to such rules as may be made by the State Government in this behalf, the State Commission may appoint such other administrative, technical and scientific staff as it may consider necessary.

(3) The salaries, allowances and conditions of service of the officers and other staff appointed under sub-section (2) shall be such as may be prescribed by the State Government.

Annual and Special Reports of State Commission

(1) The State Commission shall submit an annual report to the State Government and may at any time submit special reports on any matter which, in its opinion, is of such urgency or importance that it should not be deferred till submission of the annual report.

(2) The State Government shall cause the annual and special reports of the State Commission to be laid before each House of State Legislature where it consists of two Houses, or where such Legislature consists of one House, before that House along with a memorandum of action taken or proposed to be taken on the recommendations of the State Commission and the reasons for non-acceptance of the reactions, if any.

HUMAN RIGHTS COURTS

As per the Protection of Human Rights Act,

For the purpose of providing speedy trial of offences arising out of violation of human rights,

The State Government may, with the concurrence of the Chief Justice of the High Court, by notification, specify for each district a Court of Session to be a Human Rights Court to try the said offences.

Provided that nothing in this section shall apply if

(*a*) a Court of Session is already specified as a special court; or

(*b*) a special court is already constituted, for such offences under any other law for the time being in force.

Special Public Prosecutor

For every Human Rights Court, the State Government shall, by notification, specify a Public Prosecutor or appoint an advocate who has been in practice as an advocate for not less than seven years, as a Special Public Prosecutor for the purpose of conducting cases in that Court.

THE NATIONAL COMMISSION FOR WOMEN

The following are the functions of the National Commission for Women:

The Commission shall perform all or any of the following functions namely;

(*a*) investigate and examine all matters relating to the safeguards provided for women under the Constitution and other laws.

(*b*) Present to the Central Government, annually and at such other time as the Commission may deem fit, reports upon the working of those safeguards;

(*c*) Make in such reports recommendations for the effective the implementation of those safeguards for improv-ing the conditions of women by the Union or any State.

(*d*) Review, from time to time, the existing provisions of the Constitution and other laws affecting women and recommend amendments thereto so as to suggest remedial legislative measures to meet any lacunae, inadequacies or shortcomings in such legislations;

(*e*) take up the cases of violation of the provisions or the Constitution and of other laws relating to women with the appropriate authorities.

(*f*) Look into complaints and take *suo motu* notice of matters relating to—

(*i*) deprivation of women's rights;

(*ii*) non-implementation of laws enacted to provide protection to women and also to achieve the objective of equality and development.

(*iii*) non-compliance of policy decisions, guidelines or instructions aimed at mitigating hardships and ensuring welfare and providing relief to women, and take up the arising out of such matters, with appropriate authorities;

(*g*) call for special studies or investigations into specific problems or situations arising out of discrimination and atrocities against women and identify the constrains so as to recommend strategies for their removal;

(*h*) undertake promotional and educational research so as to suggest ways of ensuring due representation of women in all spheres and identify factors responsible for impeding their advancement, such as, lack of access to housing and basic services, inadequate support services and technologies for reducing drudgery and occupational health hazards and for increasing their productivity,

(*i*) participate and advise on the planning process of socio-economic development of women.

(*j*) Evaluate the progress of the development of women under the Union and any State;

(*k*) Inspect or cause to be inspected a jail, remand home, women's institution or other place of custody where women are kept as prisoners otherwise, and take up with the concerned authorities for remedial action, if found necessary;

(*l*) Fund litigation involving issues affecting a large body of women;

(*m*) Make periodical reports to the Government on any matter pertaining to women and in particular various difficulties under which women toil;

(*n*) any other matter which may be referred to it by the Central Government.

REFERENCES

1. Constitution of India.
2. *The Protection of Human Rights Act, 1993 with Kerala Rules*, 1998. (1998) Cochin : Suvarna Publications.
3. Mohanty, J. Human Rights Education. New Delhi : Deep& Deep publications
4. Saksena, K.P. (2000), Human Rights-Fifty years of India's Independence.
5. Mishra, P. (2000), *Human Rights in South Asia*. Delhi:Kalpaz Publications.
6. Pandey, V.P. (1999), *International Perspectives on Human Rights*. New Delhi : Mohit Publications.
7. Diwan, P., & Diwan, P. (1994), Women and Legal Protection. New Delhi : Deep and Deep Publications.

3

Human Rights Education

NEED FOR HUMAN RIGHTS EDUCATION

The inclusion of human rights education in the curriculum of schools is a derivative of a series of factors. First, the definition of human rights education varies. There is the legal definition which is drawn from the international documents that many nations have signed over the years. Some of the socialist nations offer their own political definition, which functions like a codicil attached to the international agreements. More important, teachers' and administrators' definitions of human rights education often include only those human rights which they think can be accommodated in their curriculum and classrooms.

A second determinant of human rights education is the general sense of the importance the society attaches to human rights. Where there is a genuine commitment or sense of urgency, an effort is made to include them in the curriculum., Such is the case in the Federal Republic of Germany. Human rights education receives support publicly and privately. The memory of the gross violations of human rights during the Third Reich remains. In reverse, where human rights are repeatedly curtailed, such as has been the case in Uganda and Argentina in the past, human rights education has been absent from the curriculum.

In the case of the Federal Republic of Germany, Ministry of Education guidelines state directly that human rights education is a part of the curriculum. The member states of the Council of Europe and some schools districts in the United States fall into this category. In that case, teachers may well receive suggestions on how to engage in human rights education.

Human rights education is far likely to be pursued in schools where teachers have been involved in workshops or seminars on the subject. The persuasiveness with which teachers approach the subject may depend on their own involvement in Amnesty International or other formal organizations or information groups that show a deep concern for the maintenance of human rights around the world.

The final determinant very likely is the teachers' own conviction that human rights can be effected in one's classroom. That same teachers' skills to do so becomes a critical factor. A democratic classroom where each student is respected by all others, where there reigns a caring atmosphere among students and teacher, and where the teacher designs the instructional plan with the student, and all participate in its execution, appear to be the ingredients of a classroom environment in which human rights are ever present. That kind of classroom forms a credible basis for human rights education.

As we discussed in Chapter II, the article 26 of Universal Declaration of Human Rights states that " Education shall be directed to the full development of the human personality and to the strengthening of respect of human rights and fundamental freedoms. It shall promote understanding, tolerance and friendship among all nations, racial or religious groups, and shall further the activities of the United Nations for the maintenance of peace.

Also, UNESCO's International Congress on Education for Human Rights and Democracy (1993) adopted a definition that, "Human Rights Education is a human right, a precondition for sustainable development, the civil, social, and democracy. It was also accepted that human rights education provides protection from discrimination, unfair treatment, undemocratic attitude, deterioration of cultural values, unawareness of society and environment, exploitation, bondage, human rights illiteracy, abuses of human rights at any level etc.

It is widely accepted throughout the global community that an effective human rights agenda must include strong educational component. Yet, human rights education is one of the most neglected aspects of the human rights agenda.

General Assembly Resolution 49/184 of 23 December 1994 proclaims the ten-year period beginning on 1 January 1995, the United Nations Decade for Human Rights Education. The resolution states that "human rights education should involve more than the provision of information and should constitute a comprehensive life-long process by which people at all levels in development and in all strata of society learn respect for the dignity of others and the means and methods of ensuring that respect in all societies."

Serious human rights violations caused by the upsurge of jingoism, racism, xenophobia, sexism, religious intolerance etc. show us that the world is far from civilised. Not a day goes by without someone somewhere clamouring for self-determination, free election, adequate food or housing, or, political asylum. This decade has witnessed some of the most abhorrent forms of what is euphemistically called 'ethnic cleansing', systematic rape of women, exploitation and neglect of the vulnerable sections of the society such as women, children, aged, and the indigenous people. We have also been a witness to violations which are development induced such as displacement of large sections of society, environmental degradation and health hazards.

Equally disturbing are the threats stemming from new technologies, such as cloning and genetic engineering and the scourge of new forms of diseases such as HIV+/AIDS. As an individual citizen we have a duty to discern these happenings and their dynamics. Unless we do so, we surrender power to those who claim to understand and become dependent on their interpretations and judgements.

It is contended that, to borrow a phrase from the United Nations Educational, Scientific and Cultural Organization's (UNESCO's) Constitution. It is in the minds of human beings that gross violations of human rights and prejudice have their beginning and it is in the minds of human beings that respect for human rights needs to be constructed. However this contention is only partly true. Socio-economic systems and institutions are also responsible for perpetuating injustices and denial of human rights. Therefore, human rights education should seek the necessary structural and institutional changes as well.

The principles of the 'Declaration of Human Rights' categorically state that children should enjoy special protection and be given opportunities and facilities to enable them to develop. They also reiterate that the children are entitled to the benefits of social security and to education and that they should be protected from neglect, cruelty and exploitation. It is for this purpose that everyone should be given education to learn about and respect human rights.

Education has always been a life-long and comprehensive affair. The culture of each generation must be learnt again if it is not to disappear. It should be perpetuated so as to develop a better world for posterity.

In general, the teaching of human rights as a topic has been permanently present in several teachers' seminars and conferences for educators sponsored by national and international organizations since 1948. Advocates of human rights stressed the need for everyone, everywhere, to know about his or her own rights as an essential element towards the universal implementation of human rights norms and referred to the possibility that the international community might soon launch a world publicity campaign for human rights, engaging the complementary activities of the UN system, governments and non-governmental organizations. So far, the curriculum of human rights as a subject has not received enough attention.

The purpose of education is to give people enhanced awareness, greater openness, the courage to question and perseverance in searching for solutions. The goal of initial education is to equip one with basic minimum levels of knowledge, attitudes, values and skills to start one's life journey. Historically, education is an instrument of development and a factor for social change.

Hence, the human right education must be offered to all human beings without any discrimination. However, many who are ignorant and illiterate are unaware that they are entitled to this right. Literates on many occasions fail to educate others about their rights and thereby fail in performing their social obligation to their fellow human beings.

The World Conference on Education for All, held in Jomtein, Thailand, in 1991 strongly advocated universal primary education with emphasis on education for girls and women, early childhood development and non-formal education for those who cannot go to formal schools. The statistical data of the UNICEF indicate that 40 per cent of children of school-going age do not have access to formal schooling. In Sub-Saharan Africa and South Asia, UNICEF has been focussing Curriculum reform. An ad hoc UNICEF Education advisory Committee that met in New York in July, 1991 discussed UNICEF's role and strategies to achieve education for all and decided to strengthen the education sectors at regional and national levels. This kind of education on human rights is a laudable achievement. The right to primary education is given the highest priority in the educational agenda of the world body and nation-states.

Effective human rights education is a necessary pre-condition for a healthy democratic society especially in times of crisis and threat locally, nationally and globally. The understanding and experience of human rights is an important ingredient of preparation of all young people for life in a multicultural and democratic society.

What is Human Rights Education?

Human Rights Education is education about, but also for human rights. For Example, teaching people about international law or about human rights violations such as torture is teaching about human rights. Teaching people how to respect and protect rights, is teaching for human rights. Human Rights Education is all about helping people to develop to the point where they understand human rights and where they feel that they are important and should be respected and defended.

The following list throws light on the specific needs of the Human Rights Education:

(*i*) It is the human rights education which may raise awareness about the human rights, protect from any sort of discrimination, unfair treatment and provide democratic structure, values as well as individuals freedom.

(*ii*) It contributes towards the development of global and wide perspectives, insights into the idea of international society and community.

(*iii*) It helps to make all human beings, human rights-literate.

(*iv*) It ensures essential respect for human rights in a democratic and multi-cultural society where tolerance and patience are inevitable for all.

(*v*) It protects from infringement of rights of racial, ethnic and religious group sin any country or area through inculcation of global awareness and mutual understanding among the citizens.

(*vi*) It ensures the probability of acceptance of global citizenship in all regions of the world to protect humanity based culture and democratic responsibilities.

(*vii*) It is possible to remove the fear of war in future through eradication of human rights abuses, social injustice, human selfishness and self-orientedness,

FRAMEWORK OF EDUCATIONAL POLICIES IN INDIA

The Constitution of India lays down the basic framework for the direction of the development of the country as an independent nation. The Preamble to the Constitution proclaims the resolve of the people of India to constitute a Sovereign Socialist Secular Democratic Republic that will assure to all its citizens social, economic and political justice, liberty of thought, expression, belief, faith and worship, equality of status and opportunity, and promote among them fraternity, the dignity of the individual, and the integrity of the nation.

Parts III and IV of the Constitution deal with the Fundamental Rights and Directive Principles of State Policy respectively. The human rights and fundamental freedoms laid down in the Universal Declaration of Human Rights are included in Parts III and IV and various other provisions of the Constitution.

The educational goals, policies and programmes have been spelt out within the framework of the national goals and principles laid down in the Constitution. India is a Union of States and has a federal structure. The jurisdictions of the Union and State governments have been clearly defined. In 1976, education became a concurrent subject. The formulation and implementation of educational policies have, however, always been matters of Centre-State partnership.

The Resolution on the National Policy on Education issued in 1968 prescribed a common structure of education throughout the country. The implementation of this structure, generally known as the 10+2 structure of school education, has been nearly completed throughout the country. It provided for ten years of undifferentiated general education with five years of primary, three years of upper primary and two years of secondary education. A national curriculum was also developed as a part of implementation of the new structure.

The study of one to three languages at different stages, science, mathematics and social studies/social sciences, besides art education, work experience and health and physical education were made compulsory in this framework. At the higher secondary stage (grades XI- XII), differentiated courses were introduced and the student initiated into the specialized study of a few subjects of her/his choice along with core courses. The National Policy on Education (NPE) adopted by Parliament in 1986 visualized the national curriculum framework with a common core as a basis for building the national system of education.

The NPE (1986), with its stress on the national curriculum with a common core, has further strengthened human rights education by making it an integral part of the curriculum in every subject and at all stages of school education. Most of the 'common core' elements laid down in the Policy are related to one or other dimension of education for human rights and democracy. These elements are 'the history of India's freedom movement, the constitutional obligations and other contents essential to nurture national identity.

It has been laid down that these elements will cut across subject areas and will be designed to promote values such as India's common cultural heritage, egalitarianism, democracy and secularism, equality of the sexes, protection of the environment, removal of social barriers, observance of the small family norm and inculcation of the scientific temper. All educational programmes will be carried on in strict conformity with secular values.

'To promote equality', the Policy lays down, 'it will be necessary to provide for equal opportunity not only in access, but also in the conditions for success. Besides, awareness of the inherent equality of all will be created through the core curriculum. The purpose is to remove prejudices and complexes transmitted through the social environment and the accident of birth. The Policy also lays stress on the 'combative role' of education in eliminating obscurantism, religious fanaticism, violence, superstition and fatalism. Part IV of the Policy deals with education for equality, education of Scheduled Castes and Scheduled Tribes and other educationally backward sections and areas, minorities and the handicapped.

The way in which the courses and teaching at the school level are structured does not provide for the study of specific issues and concerns as separate areas. In any case, issues of human rights are integrally connected with various other issues which are among major concerns of school curriculum as a whole as well as of the curricula in various school subjects.

They cannot be separated from issues relating to secularism, national integration, gender bias, protection of the environment and many others which are among the major concerns of curricula in languages/literature, social sciences, sciences and other subjects. The approach of integrating into the existing school subjects does not preclude activities and projects which are specifically and exclusively focused on human rights and democracy.

Principles of Human Rights Education

As reported by Flowers (1998), ten principles of Human Rights Education are listed below:

1. Provide open-minded examination of human rights issues and concerns with ample opportunities for participants to arrive at positions different from those of the presenter.
2. Avoid too much focus on human rights abuses. Emphasize human rights as a positive value system and a standard to which everyone is entitled.
3. Include an international /global dimension to the human rights topic being discussed-how it manifests itself at home and abroad.
4. Connect every issue or topic to relevant articles of the Universal Declaration of Human Rights. Make this connection explicit rather than implicit or assumed. Keep in mind that linking every issue with the Universal Declaration of Human Rights is important.
5. Emphasize on the belief that the individual can make a difference and substantiate with examples who have done so in the course of time.
6. Include action dimension that provides participants with opportunities to act on their beliefs and under-standings. These actions should address problems both at home and elsewhere around the globe.
7. Be responsive to concerns related to cultural diversity. Methods and activities should reflect a variety of perspectives such as gender, race, religion, cultural and national traditions.
8. Keep lecturing to minimum. Use participatory methods for learning such as discussion, role playing debates, games, simulations and case studies.
9. Keep both content, learning process and the class environment in mind. It is difficult to engage participants in examining issues

related to human rights and justice if the learning environment does not demonstrate respect of justice and human dignity.

10. Connect people's lived experiences directly to abstract concepts dealt within human rights education and legal documents.

HUMAN RIGHTS EDUCATION IN INDIA

Programmes for promotion of human rights education have been instituted in almost all countries in Europe, North America, a few countries in Latin America and Africa. But precious little has been done in this regard in Asian countries. This is despite the fact that in India and other South Asian countries the problem of human rights education has colossal and complex dimensions. Here, a vast majority of the people do not even enjoy the right to education, which is one of the primary human right. As per the 1991 census some 328.9 million illiterate people live in India. The problem, though serious, can be turned into an advantage because our programme for the removal of adult literacy can very easily be used to inculcate human rights dimension.

Despite many of the shortcomings of the present educational system in the country, human rights education must begin there. With this in view the National Human Rights Commission (NHRC) has been working over the years with the Department of Education, Ministry of Human Resource Development, the National Council of Education Research and Training (NCERT) and the National Council for Teacher Education (NCTE).

In 1980, the University Grants Commission (UGC) constituted a committee under the chairmanship of Justice S. M. Sikri to consider ways and means of promoting human rights education in India. The committee in its report entitled ' Human Rights Education at All Levels', suggested different approaches at different levels of education. At school level human rights value should best be inculcated through stories, visual aids, exhibition and such other methods. At higher levels these values and ideas can be taught through book and other lessons. The committee felt that even graduate students in science, commerce, medicine and engineering should be exposed to certain perspectives of human rights.

In 1997, the UGC constituted a standing Committee on Human Rights Education to start post-graduate course in the universities and to deal with matters relating to the organising of seminars, workshops and symposia at the university level. The Committee has been able to give direction to teaching and research in this comparatively new academic endeavour. The Standing Committee approved proposals for starting certificate, diploma and degree courses in human rights at the Indira Gandhi National Open University (IGNOU), New Delhi; the University of Mumbai, Andhra University, Waltair; Manipur University, Jamia Millia Islamia, New Delhi; Saurashtra University, Rajkot; Jawaharlal University, New Delhi; Nagpur University and Aligarh Muslim University.

The most important aspect of the UGC's initiative has been the emphasis on going beyond mere intellectual exercise. It envisages linkages between colleges/universities and NGOs. It expects the students to do field work as part of the course. This is a vital development in the mainstreaming of human rights education.

Elementary Level

In India, the *varna* system under which slaves and Sudras traditionally were placed at the lowest rung to serve people of the other three varnas was a stumbling-block to their progress. People of this class were forbidden to learn the Vedas and were rarely initiated as disciples, and their exclusion was justified on grounds of Karma and fate. Ekalavya, a hunter portrayed in the *Mahabharata*, was effectively prevented from learning the art of archery from Drona, the teacher of the Pandavas, as Drona made him sacrifice his thumb as *guru dakshina*. Belonging to an un-touchable people, the hunter was left with no choice.

Offering education to people who had traditionally been excluded did not seem to rulers a redressal of injustice. This situation continues in some places in India. India has accepted elementary education as the basic need of every individual. The Constitution directs the State to provide free education to all children in the age group of 6-14 years. The rate of expansion of elementary education is an index of the national pursuit of the goal of universalization of elementary education.

Importance

From the child's early years, education for human rights is both practical as well as necessary. Pre-school and early elementary education can highlight a sense of common humanity among children. An important aim of education is to develop positive attitudes and values in children while they are young. Advances made in the Psychology of Learning and Instruction have shown that it is possible to expose young children to these issues as part of their preparation for adulthood and future citizenship. Even the curriculum of the elementary level today exposes children to local, regional and national cultures.

In a country like ours it is all the more important to expose children to the concept of one World and Human Rights at this stage because many children do not go beyond the elementary level. It is important to have a proper, developed programme for the students of the elementary stage. They are entering school for the first time, and secondly, right at this stage they start developing broader perspectives because of being exposed to reading and interpersonal interaction. This, in turn, brings numerous changes in their attitudes and behaviour.

So when we prepare a programme for the students of this age group we must take their developmental characteristics into account. Our aims, objectives, content and methods of their education depend on this. Children at the elementary stage enjoy all sorts of activities which become a source of joy for them and they look forward to doing it.

At this stage, speech becomes an important tool for group interaction and for sharing experiences. There is also a shift from ego-centric to socially-oriented speech. This is the time when concepts of right and wrong and new standards of morality take shape. Once these concepts are internalised they can be applied to a broader variety of situations. When we import Human Rights Education at the elementary level we will have to take into account all these factors as they will make our work many times easier.

A little older children in the elementary school develop interest in reading story books, especially books which have many illustrations; books that contain stories about heroes and heroines; and stories from mythology, especially The Ramayana and The Mahabharata. They like to watch programmes on T.V and like to hear the radio, too. All these can be used as means for developing international understanding. They can also be helped to develop positive attitudes towards their own group and towards people who are culturally different from themselves. But the teacher has to be very careful because instructions at this stage should enable the child to develop healthy attitudes, as free as possible from prejudices.

Primary Level

On the first day of school, it's time to start setting the foundations for a classroom which functions with respect for each child, and with children respecting each other.

It may be apparent when you look at lunches and discover that one child eats bread or noodles each day, while another hates it. There is the chance to explain that people have different opinions or tastes, look different from each other, and that you respect these differences.

Make children aware of the many areas in a school experience where you emphasize the rights of each person. The teachable moments come at unexpected times. Use them! Within a few weeks you will be ready to introduce the children to the Universal Declaration of Human Rights—An Adaptation for Children (by Rocha.R and Roth.O United Nations Publications, 1989)

The use of big words with children is almost always a captivating experience.

Start with the word *universal.* Most children know the word universe, and can figure out that universal means everybody on our planet Earth. Ask what the word *rights* means. Have children look at each child in the group and, discuss the outstanding features as you together discover the range of different skin colours, hair, size, etc.

If your class is a more homogeneous group, have children check out noses or ears and it will be evident that they are each unique individuals. It is the time to bring out a Book like, PEOPLE (Spier. P Doubleday and Co.,1980). It gives an idea of differences in the four billion people on Earth in wonderful ways. Pictures in books, discussions, the materials in your classroom, the pictures on the wall, and your responses all need to show respect during work and play times. Children will soon know that each person, child, or adult is important, needs to be respected and has rights.

You and your children are now ready to write a Declaration of Human Rights. It may be one based on the Universal Declaration of

Human Rights (UDHR) or it may be one which reflects the rights of children in your classroom. You can start the class on rights in October or November.

A possible beginning is to ask each child to pretend he/she is writing the Universal Declaration, and to think and suggest a right which seems important to her/him. As a right is offered, the whole body of children should discuss it, agree or disagree, and, when a consensus is reached, the accepted right is put on a long sheet of paper. Use the children's language for a meaningful Declaration.

Continue the list for as many days as there are ideas, with the deadline being Human Rights Day, December 10th, the anniversary of the creation of the Universal Declaration of Human Rights (1948). You can conduct a ceremony on this day.

Study of Different Subjects

The main relevant subjects at the lower primary stage are environmental studies and language (s). The curriculum in environmental studies aims at promoting knowledge and understanding of the natural and physical and also the social and cultural environment. Beginning with the study of those aspects of the environment which are within the immediate experience of the child, the scope is extended to include the district, state, country and world. Narratives and biographies of men and women from the history of India and of the world, India's freedom struggle and certain aspects of Indian Constitution can be included.

In the language curriculum the focus should be on the development of personal qualities of compassion, tolerance and sympathy. This can be done through an appropriate selection of stories, poems and other literary forms.

The human rights dimension in this course has its main focus on the following:

1. Developing knowledge and respect for the diversity and variety in the Ethnic composition and culture, language, religion, customs and ways of living in India and the world;
2. Developing knowledge about men and women from different places through the ages who have struggled for justice, human brotherhood and human equality;

3. Developing an understanding of the vision of independent India as it evolved during the struggle for freedom;
4. Promoting a general understanding of national goals and main features of Fundamental Rights, Directive Principles and Fundamental Duties;
5. Promoting concern about deprivation, poverty, disease, illiteracy and inequalities; and
6. Developing knowledge and concern about the environment and its degradation.

In the upper elementary stages the major subject areas relevant to Human Rights Education are Social Studies, Sciences and Languages. In India, the guidelines are prepared by NCERT which provide the general framework for the syllabus in different Social Studies subjects like History, Geography and Civics. The course in History at this stage deals mainly with Indian history and in general with the history of world civilization. While teaching these lessons, stress can be laid on developing an understanding of and appreciation for India's cultural heritage, its composite nature, richness as well as variety. We should also emphasise that in spite of all this diversity and variety, we are humans having consideration for each other's rights.

Through History lessons the teacher can help in developing an understanding of the struggle for freedom and the ideals that it embodied for reconstructing Indian society, polity and economy on the principles of democracy, secularism and egalitarianism which are integral to the promotion of human rights and to make students to identify cases of observation and violation of human rights.

The relevance of the geography course which deals with the geography of different continents and of a few selected countries in each continent lies in bringing into sharp focus the variety of ways of living in different parts of India and of the world and developing an appreciation for this variety.

The course in Civics containing topics on national integration and democracy can help in promoting well informed and intelligent citizenship for effective participation in the affairs of the community. At primary stage, values of democracy, socialism, secularism, justice, equality and national integration can be inculcated in the children. Civics introduces the study of Fundamental Rights, Directive

Principles and Fundamental Duties which have been enshrined in the Indian constitution.

The language classes can be effectively use to the following:

(a) Develop in the children the ability to communicate clearly ideas, opinions and arguments concerning the issues at hand.

(b) While the children are asked to write stories and essays, the teacher can help to develop the ability to collect information and to analyse and synthesize it for use in formulating decisions and writing e.g. stories where the students feel that a human right has been violated or how they can help in strengthening a particular human right.

(c) Ability to participate in citizenship action at their own level e.g. They can use their communication skills to collect funds for victims of natural calamities at home or abroad or for any other tragedy that has taken place.

(d) The teacher can help change the attitude of the children so that they develop an attitude of acceptance of other children from different ethnic groups and tolerance of difference in opinions, beliefs and customs.

The course in science has been introduced as an un diversified subject at this stage. The objective of teaching science has been to inculcate a national outlook and there by help in critical observation and doing away with prejudices based on narrow considerations, of caste, sex or religion. The guidelines also emphasise the objective of promoting understanding of the process and problems of areas related to agriculture, health and nutrition, environmental protection, energy and material resources and more importantly develop a scientific attitude to live more effectively as a responsible citizen.

Secondary Level

The secondary stage is more advanced than the elementary stage. Knowledge should now be presented more systematically and the students should be encouraged to develop the capacity for action.Affective development should continue to be encouraged, but greater emphasis should now be placed on the exercise of critical and reflective faculties. Individual and social behaviour should be developed in a more analytical and critical way.

Students should reflect upon the values underlying behaviour. The teacher should encourage the students to explore major contemporary world problems. They should begin by analysing complete situations and then making a transition to general and abstract considerations and finally moving towards organized action.

The Secondary school teachers should enable students to work in a democratic manner. They should get themselves enrolled with local, national and international committees so as to promote respect for human rights, the establishment of justice and the safeguarding of peace.

The organization, spirit and atmosphere of the school are essential components of education on human rights at the secondary level. The principles of human rights should ideally be reflected in all the daily operations of school life and in the relations between teachers and pupils as well as between members of the two groups. If students have some voice in the affairs of the school and in the planning of their programmes, they gain valuable experience, not only in exercising their rights but also in handling responsibilities.

Abstract principles of rights and duties should be integrated in terms of real situations. Once we go through the secondary school curriculum, we will find that almost every subject in the curriculum has something to contribute to the sum and substance of knowledge and experience. But there are more topics in history, civics and literature which help in transaction of Human Rights.

Generally Literary works raise questions of values and rights. Sometimes, they present real or imaginary situations involving conflict. A writer whatever his/her artistic ambition, cannot avoid dealing with human dramas, novels or religious and philosophical works which describe or reflect the social scene. Sometimes, the authors write about demand for certain rights and freedoms and of the struggle to obtain them.

Instruments of rights such as the Universal Declaration of Human Rights and the International Covenants could provide the material for lessons in analysis and comprehension, or a class might be assigned some of the articles of the universal declaration for essay subjects.

Students can made their own versions of the Universal Declaration, or of the Declaration of the Rights of the Child. In studying works of literature, students can recognize the social relations and contradictions upon which conflict are based; how people long for and aspire to a decent life of peace, freedom and social justice.

In a **language** class students can be asked to write poems or essays in which they depict certain evils in society. The students in this exercise first talk about the work done by children, men and women. The teacher can help the students to highlight the fact that men and women are equal and women have a right to get equal status in society but regarding work, children are different hence child labour is to be avoided. Children are to be given proper dignity. The students learn that they have a right to opportunity, right to education and the right to live as equal human beings as others.

Social Science help the students to analyse the contemporary scene in the light of past events and trends and to anticipate to some extent, the course of development in international relations. In the secondary school, Human Rights can be taught in the context and understanding of the following areas:

1. The United Nations
2. The world today; east-west problems, armaments, events and personalities in international affairs.
3. Studies of individual countries
4. The family and society; economic, political and cultural inter-dependence.
5. Family life, school and community.
6. Community, country and state.

The study of problems faced by the world may lead to an enquiry into the work of United Nations and its agencies in helping to solve such problems through International co-operation.

In the **Civics Course**, children are often required to make a detailed study of human rights and duties as represented in their own country's contribution or other bodies of law. Familiarity with the terms of various documents makes a viable introduction to the study of United Nations Declaration, Covenants and Conventions concerned with human rights, enabling the pupils to move naturally from consideration of national standards to critical analysis of the rights affirmed for all.

History covers such topics as the origins and growth of democratic thinking and organization, the development of the United Nations, the growth of trade unions, social reforms and independence movements. The topic of the Industrial Revolution, embracing its impact on countries outside Europe, might be linked with a study of the International Labour Organization and its efforts to ensure just and equitable conditions for all workers and to abolish forced labour and other abuses of human dignity and freedom.

A study of slavery might lead to a consideration of why it is necessary to include in history, articles in the Universal Declaration of Human Rights condemning this practice. Historical Figures such as, Anne Frank (Netherlands); Mahatma Gandhi (India); Martin Luther King (USA) : Andrei Sakharov (USSR) etc. can be covered.

Geography helps to foster a relationship between students and their own country, students learn about the environment and living conditions of different people, their specific cultures, their economic situation and the interdependence between countries. They will also learn about the nature of underdevelopment in certain sectors of the industrialized regions and in third world countries.

The course in **Economics** at this stage deals mainly with the study of the Indian economy with emphasis on the twin objectives of economic development and social justice. Among the objectives of this course is the inculcation of passion for social justice and an urge to resist exploitation in any form by men or by the State.

Science Education lays stress on the development of a scientific temper, the cultivation of social ethical, moral and aesthetic values, and development of 'sensitivity to possible uses and misuses of science and concern for a clean environment and preservation of the ecosystem'. It attempts to relate the concepts and principles of science with agriculture, communication, industry, energy and material resources, health, environment and social forestry. Health issues are a good way to introduce human rights in this subject. For example, students have a right to health care, but also the responsibility to respect their own and other people's health. There are great opportunities for cross-departmental teaching. For example, a biology lesson examining myths about racial superiority can inform students to make better judgements in a parallel study of racism in history.

In **Biology,** the study of transmission and the distribution of characteristics and the relationship of hereditary and cultural factors are appropriate parts of the subject matter and can serve to combat racial prejudice. Science can also include teaching of health and disease and the work done by World Health Organization in controlling diseases.

In **Physical Science**, the history of industrial revolution, inventions which enhanced such revolution and the relation of the revolution with human rights can be included. Many examples can be taken to show the role played by computer technology, electronics, nuclear physics, chemistry, bio-chemistry, in national economies and in modern military engineering. Priority should be given to the moral duty and social responsibility of scientists and technicians for the humanitarian application of their findings.

In **Mathematics** there are potentialities in the use of data of an international character. Statistics can be used to hide or reveal human rights abuses. The maths teacher can also show students how to critically interpret figures which appear in newspapers. The skills of elementary statistics, graphing and the interpretation of data might well be exercised on information about such matter as food and populations, agricultural and industrial output, expenditures on armaments and on education and other topics that have a bearing on progress in attaining basic human rights.

Knowledge and appreciation of the **Arts** of other countries rarely fail to create some bond of empathy and understanding between peoples which may strengthen the sense of responsibility for universal Human Rights, Studies of the history or art, or of the lives and achievements of artists and musicians raise questions of freedom of expression, economic freedom for the creative artist and the problem of patronage for the artists in general, or the preservation of art treasures and monuments- all topics which are likely to be readily discussed and which can help to convey the meaning of the universality of rights.

Language skills can be used to study interesting current themes from other countries. For example, a short text about action against racism in England could be used to teach English vocabulary. The aim would be to give students an understanding of the human rights issues facing people in all countries, as well as knowledge of a foreign language. If available, foreign language press or literature is helpful for this teaching style, but not essential.

Foreign Language classes are opportunities for students to talk and discuss. They will be most motivated to discuss when the topic is one on which there are different opinions. Questions of discrimination or of gender equality make good discussion topics. Students can also enjoy role play. Foreign language classes are also a chance for students to correspond with students in other countries. They could ask about political systems, current social questions, the treatment of minorities and any other questions relating to human rights.

Higher Secondary Level

This stage marks the initiation of students into the specialized study of subjects of their choice. The NCERT has recommended a core course of General Studies, compulsory for students of all streams. This course is particularly relevant to education for human rights and democracy.

Besides themes like ' Science, Technology and Society', Environment, Society and Development', Global Issues of Human Survival', this course recommends the study of human rights in historical perspective, the Universal Declaration of Human Rights, human rights conventions, the present state of human rights, racism and apartheid and struggle against them, unequal international economic relations and problems of world economic development; social structure and social justice dealing mainly with the basic components of Indian society, social and economic inequalities, economic exploitation and atrocities against weaker sections, child labour, status of women in Indian society and dynamics of the quest for equality; and the study of the challenges of communalism, revivalism, casteism and various kinds of chauvinism to India's national unity. This course also recommends the need for identifying local problems within the broad framework of these themes.

Contemporary world history provides a historical perspective for the study of contemporary world problems including the study of the Universal Declaration of Human Rights. The political science courses focus on the study of the problems of Indian democracy and various contemporary world problems.

Sociology, one of the social science disciplines which is a part of the school curriculum at this stage in some States, helps to promote an objective understanding of social reality and specific issues and problems of Indian society, including inequalities and the quest for equality. It provides broad human rights and cultural perspectives for the understanding of interactive processes in society, the pluralist nature of most modern societies, the problems and rights of ethnic and religious minorities and, in the Indian context, problems of scheduled castes and tribes, and other depressed sections of society.

Science course at this stage are important in bringing out the unscientific nature of racist views and theories. It is stressed that all humans are members of the same species.

METHODS OF TEACHING HUMAN RIGHTS

In addition to acquiring the skills to foster critical thinking, beginning teachers would need to learn numerous methods thought to be critical in human rights teaching. They should learn how to lead and participate in open discussion; involve students in the creation of curricula; establish classroom climates conducive to equal participa-tion by all students; encourage expression of opinions about social and economic problems and government's actions to resolve them; emphasize student opportunities to exercise judgments and solve problems.

Teachers would learn about the need for a staged introduction of human rights concepts from preschool through adulthood; and how at each stage to connect them with personal situations and experiences. Some of the methods of teaching that can be used in the teaching of human rights are described below:

USEFUL TEACHING METHODS

1. Role play

A role-play is a little drama played by the students. It is mostly improvised. It aims to bring to life circumstances or events which are unfamiliar to students. Role plays can improve understanding of a situation and encourage empathy towards those who are in it. For example, in a role play about a robbery, students, by acting the part of the victim, can gain insight into what it is like to be the victim of crime.

Procedure

- Identify the issue which the role play will illustrate. For example, the right to property (Article 17 of the UDHR,)

- Decide on the situation, the problem, and who the characters are. For example, if the class are studying the right to property, they could think of a situation where someone might be deprived of their apartment, maybe because of the community group they belong to, or because of a lack of legislation. With the students, decide how many students will do the role play, how many will be observers. Encourage shy students to be involved.

Also, decide how the role play will work. For example, it could be

- told as a story, where a narrator sets the scene and other students tell the rest of the event from the point of view of "their" character.
- a drama, where the characters interact, inventing dialogue on the spot.
- a mock trial, where the students pretend to be witnesses testifying in a court.

Now allow two minutes for students to think about the situation and their roles. If the furniture needs to be re-arranged to make space, do it now.

Students Performance

During the role play, it might be useful to stop the action at a critical point to ask the participants and the observers about what is happening. For example, in a role play about violence, ask the students if they can think of a way that the situation could be resolved peacefully, then ask the participants to play out those possible endings.

After the role play, it is important that students think about what just took place, so that it is not just an activity, but is also a learning experience.

Role-plays need to be used with sensitivity. The teacher needs to respect the feelings of individuals and the social structure of the class. (For example, a role play about ethnic minorities needs careful handling if there are ethnic minorities in the classroom, so that students belonging to them will not feel exposed or marginalised.)

2. Brainstorming

Brainstorming is a way to encourage creativity and to generate a lot of ideas very quickly. It can be used for solving a specific problem or answering a question. For example, the class could start a study of the right to citizenship by brainstorming answers to the question "what reasons do you think a government might use for taking away someone's citizenship?"

When to use it?

To find a solution to a problem: For example, after an "ncident" involving conflict between students, ask the class to brainstorm all the possible non-violent solutions.

To introduce a new subject: Brainstorm everything that the students already know about the subject. This is a good way to arouse their interest and find out what they already know.

As a quick creative exercise. For example, brainstorm possible endings for an unfinished story.

Procedure

Decide on the issue you want to brainstorm. Form it into a question which will have many possible answers. Write the question where everyone can see it. For example: "In what ways can we improve our classroom?"

Ask students to contribute their ideas. Write the ideas where everyone can see them. These should be single words or short phrases. Tell the students that in a brainstorm they can't comment on each other's ideas until the end, or repeat ideas which have already been said.

Encourage everyone to contribute, but do *NOT* move around the class in a circle, or force students to think of an idea (this is likely to discourage creativity). Don't judge the ideas as you write them down. If possible, ask a student to write them. Only give your own ideas if it is necessary to encourage students. If a suggestion is unclear, ask the person to clarify it, or suggest a clarification and check that they agree to it.

Write down *every* new suggestion. Often, the most creative or outrageous suggestions are the most useful and interesting! Stop the brainstorm when ideas are running out. NOW, you can go through the suggestions, asking for comments. (Based on the Amnesty International Human Rights Network).

3. Forming Pairs and Groups

Dividing the class into pairs or groups gives students more opportunities for participating and cooperating. Pairs and groups can be useful to generate a lot of ideas very quickly, or to help the class to think about an abstract concept in terms of their own experience. For example, if you were studying the right to life, you could give pairs or groups five minutes to decide "Is it ever right to kill someone?", before returning to the whole-class plenary for further discussion.

Organisation

When organizing the groups, ask yourself questions like: Do I want to divide students according to ability? Do I want to combine the sexes? Do I want friends to work together? Sometimes groups can be chosen at random. For example, by role number, or by the first letter of their name, or other non-obvious criteria.

If the tables and chairs are fixed to the floor, students can form groups by turning around in their seats to face the students behind.

If a group will be together for more than a few minutes, it might be necessary to have a chairperson and someone to write notes. The group would need to decide who will do these jobs.

Organising the Class

Explain the task clearly. Seat students where they can see each other. Tell the students how long they have for the task.

When the pairs or groups are working, the teacher can:

- Stand back, but be available.
- Do not interrupt, unless a group has misunderstood what it is supposed to be doing.
- Spread her attention between groups.
- Allow group and pair discussions to flow, only intervene if asked to by the group.
- Groups often need encouragement to get them going.

Reporting back: It might be necessary for groups to report their work to the whole class. This might involve reporting a decision, summarizing a discussion, or giving information about how the group functioned. This sort of debriefing can be very useful for both the teacher and the class for improving group-work technique. If the groups will need to report back, they need to know this at the start so that they can select someone for this task.

Evaluation: Ask students whether the activity was useful, and what they learned.

If there is a negative response, ask the students how they would organise the activity. Use their ideas.

4. Discussion

Discussions are a good way for the teacher and the students to discover what their attitudes are about human rights issues. This is very important for teaching human rights, because as well as knowing the facts, students also need to explore and analyse issues for themselves. Discussions are also an opportunity to practice listening, speaking in turn and other group skills which are important for respecting other people's rights.

In order to have an open discussion, it is important to have an atmosphere of trust and mutual respect in the classroom. One way to help create a congenial environment is to have students develop some Rules for Discussion..

Ask the students if they want their classroom to be a place where they feel free to express themselves and to learn through discussion with each other. Suggest that it might be possible for the class to reach a common understanding of the protocol for listening and speaking.

Ask the class to think of some principles for classroom discussion which they think everyone should follow. Write all of these suggestions where everyone can see them. After the students have brainstormed for a while, look and see if there are any suggestions which could be combined, and invite the class to discuss or comment.

Some of the suggestions are

- listen to the person who is speaking
- only one person speaks at a time
- raise your hand to be recognized if you want to say something
- don't interrupt when someone is speaking
- don't laugh when someone is speaking (unless they make a joke!)
- encourage everyone to participate

Suggest that the class agree by consensus to obey the rules which they have listed. They are then responsible for applying the rules to themselves and to other members of the class.

5. Projects

Projects are the independent investigation of topics by students over an extended period, ending in a final product. Projects are useful for teaching human rights because they:

1. Help students to see links between separate subjects and between their school studies and the outside world.

2. Give students practice at organizing themselves for action, planning their own time and working to a schedule.

3. Allow students to take control of their own learning, with the guidance of the teacher.

4. Create opportunities for students to interact with each other and with diverse people in the community outside the school.

5. Give students practice at presenting and defending their own findings and opinions in public—an important skill for promoting human rights.

Procedure

Projects have distinct stages. Throughout, the emphasis is on allowing students to take responsibility for their own study.

The topic or problem. These can be identified by the teacher, and presented to the class as choices, or chosen directly by the class, For example, "Are refugees in our town treated well?" The question needs to be specific to avoid students getting lost' in the subject.

Planning. Teachers and students need to decide when the project will begin, how long it will take, what resources will be used, where these can be found, whether students will work alone or in groups, on the same or different topics, and so on. It is very important to discuss at this stage how the project will be concluded

Implementation: Project work builds a lot of skills very quickly. e.g., an investigative project about local health care might involve visits, interviews, reading, taking photographs, collecting statistics, and analysing data. A creative project might involve technical knowledge, such as how to work a video camera, and artistic skill, such as banner/poster-making. The best projects combine academic, social and creative skills to involve all the students' abilities. The teacher can help during this stage by answering questions or offering advice, but the students are responsible for doing the work.

The product: This might be a report, a film, an exhibition, an audio tape, a lecture, a painting, a poem.....It is a good idea if the product records not only the students' findings but also the different stages of the project and the students' own feelings about the topic being studied.

The product can be presented to the class, or to a wider audience. For example, a project about poverty in your area might interest the local newspaper or the municipal authorities might want to know the results of a project about environmental damage.

Evaluation: Because projects are often multi-disciplinary, several teachers may need to give assessments of the product. Marking needs to reflect the diverse skills which have been used during the project, and should not only focus on academic criteria.

6. Questioning

All teachers already use questions everyday. Often, they are questions such as 'open' questions such as. "what did I just say?" These are used to control the class. Other questions which are used a lot are so-called 'closed' questions. They have only one correct answer and are used to test knowledge. In discussions, the questions you ask are very important for encouraging participation and analysis, even with very young children.

Here are some examples of 'open' questions which you could use.

Hypothetical questions: "What would you do/think if......?" These help students to imagine situations and stimulate thought.

Speculating: "How might we help to solve this problem?"

Encouraging/supporting: 'That's interesting, what happened next?" These draw out students' own experience and views.

Opinion seeking: "What do you think or feel about...?" This tells students that their opinion is important and interesting for you.

Probing: "Why do you think that?" If asked in a non-aggressive way, this can help students to think deeply and justify/analyse their opinions.

Clarifying/summarising: "Am I right to say that you think.....?" Summarising what a student said and checking if you understand it will help other students to think whether they agree with what is being said.

Identifying agreement: "Do most of us agree that.....?" This can provoke discussion or can come at the end, where, by using a question like "Have we finished that part...?", you can agree to move on to the next topic.

Try to remember to avoid leading or trick questions such as "X is correct, isn't it?" This discourage participation. Asking too many questions at once or asking ambiguous questions should also be avoided. And remember, an occasional nod, a smile or even just sitting on the same level as the class, will improve the responses you get!

7. Buzz session

A "buzz session" can be used to change the pace of the lesson. For example, after a long presentation by the teacher. It is an opportunity to talk in pairs or threes.

Procedure: Based on the previous knowledge of the students, the teacher may pose a set of complicated problems or tasks. Tell students that for five minutes they can react to what has just been said or shown. They can say how they feel, what they think or ask each other questions about things they didn't understand.

Allot a fixed time for students to discuss the problem in small groups. Clear instructions may be given so that discussions are productive. The efficiency of such a session would be enhanced by the teacher moving around and getting a feel of active discussion without interrupting.

Once the small groups finalise the solutions to the problem, the representative of the group reports back to the teacher. The teacher has to compile all these reports and provide her judgement to the students. This is called buzz session because groups buzz *like Bees* while discussing the problem.

8. Activities based on pictures

i) Drawing

Drawing can be used in the classroom to develop observation and cooperation skills, imagination, feelings of empathy for people in the pictures, or to get to know the other members of the class. Drawing is useful when teaching human rights because the work of the class can be exhibited in the school to communicate human rights values to other students. Some ideas for using drawing are given below.

Procedure: Collect pictures, photographs, drawings on different subjects from newspapers, magazines or books. Ask the students to work in pairs. Give every student a picture and some drawing materials. Tell the students not to show their picture to their partner.

Each student describes his or her picture to a partner, who has to try to draw it from the description alone. After ten minutes, the pair reverse roles. Because of the time limit, the drawings will be quite simple. The important thing is the describing, not the drawing. The students then take it in turns to compare their drawings with the original pictures. Ask them if anything important was left out? What? Why? Where students have a formal art lesson, there may be opportunities to create posters or artworks which express a concern for or a commitment to human rights.

ii) Pictures and Photographs

Because pictures or photographs appear to be the same to all viewers, but are actually interpreted by us all in different ways, they can be extremely effective for showing students how we all see things differently.

Procedure: Give students in pairs a picture to look at. Give the pairs five minutes to write down all the questions they have about it. Ask them to choose the four most important questions. The picture could be related to a topic which you or another teacher is teaching.

Now ask each pair to show their picture and their four most important questions to the neighbouring pair. Give them ten minutes to work together to find answers to all of their questions. Ask them to make two lists:

1. questions they can't find an answer to.
2. questions with a possible answer.

For the questions with a possible answer it is important that they write down WHY they chose this answer. For example, if they think that a child in a picture is from a cold country, what clues were there in the picture which helped them to decide this?

Make a display of all the pictures, questions and answers. Ask the students to look at everyone else's picture, questions and answers, and make further comments where necessary. Leave a space where teachers, parents or other students can also comment and contribute their own ideas about the pictures.

iii) Cartoons and Comics

Cartoons and comics have powerful influences on young people. They can entertain and inform or encourage prejudices and stereotypes. They can be used in the classroom in many different ways. For example, you can prepare for a discussion about violence in the media by asking students to count how many episodes of violence occur in cartoons and comics in a week. Cartoons drawn by the students themselves can also be used as a way to communicate human rights issues to the rest of the school.

Procedure: Take cartoons/strips from newspapers, magazines, comics and advertisements which relate to the subject being studied. For example, violence, intolerance, or racism. Ask students to discuss them in groups. Then ask:

- What is your first emotional response?
- What is the message of the cartoon or comic story?
- Are the images effective in telling the story, expressing the point of view, making people think about the issues?
- Does it criticize an idea, or a group of people?
- Does it include stereotypes or prejudices towards a particular group of people, such as women, ethnic groups, refugees, people with disabilities?
- Is it serious, humorous or ironic? How does this contribute to the message? or

Ask students to choose a human rights issue and draw a cartoon or comic strip about it. Ask them to try to present this topic in the most powerful way, so that the pictures will make people think about the issues. Display the results.

9. Using Mass Media

i) Using Newspapers

The media are essential for enabling information to circulate in a democratic society. However sometimes we find subjective reporting using stereotypes and prejudices. Identifying and analysing prejudice in newspapers prepares students to identify it and oppose it in every day situations. This sort of activity also improves students' communication skills.

Procedure: Choose a current rights issue which receives a lot of media coverage in your country, for example, the treatment of minorities. Alternatively, choose a trend which lies behind several different stories, such as intolerance.

Divide the class into groups of four or five. Give each group at least one story from local or national newspapers about the chosen topic. If necessary, the same report can be used by all the groups. Reports from different newspapers about the same event are good for comparison.

Ask each group to discuss some questions from the following list. Select questions appropriate to the reports being used, or invent others:

- Does the title of the report suggest its view on the issue?
- What is your first impression of the situation described? Does anyone seem to be at fault? If so, who?
- Are direct accusations made against anyone? If so, list them.
- Is any proof offered to support the allegations?
- Which words do you think are the most important in creating your impression of the report?
- What impressions, if any, are given of ordinary people's views on the issue?
- What is the attitude of people in authority? For example, social workers, police, officials and so on.

You could also ask students to bring in interesting articles or stories they have found in newspapers. In this way, a class collection can be formed, which can be used as a basis for class discussions. Parents can become involved by helping students to identify interesting articles.

ii) Video

Organizations like the Council of Europe and Amnesty International have produced video cassettes for classroom use Parts of the TV News or a documentary can also be useful. Here are some suggestions to remember when using videos:

If students process the information received from videos, they are more likely to remember it. For example, they could use their imagination to write a diary from the point of view of a character seen in the video, or use the video as the basis for a discussion.

10. Re-creating Information

A good way to internalise and understand information is to re-create it in another form. For example, to listen to a story and then tell it in pictures. Students will have to identify the most important part of the information and decide how to re-create it. The student has to decide, "I'm going to do it this way because..."

This technique helps to develop the imagination, as well as skills of observation, selection and reasoning.

Procedure: With the students, choose a source such as a story, a picture, a poem, a cartoon or a film. For example, if the class is studying the right to be with one's family, a picture of a refugee child could be used. Students read, look at or listen carefully to the original version. They decide which parts of the story to transfer to the new medium, and explain their choices. If you are using a picture, then they will need to imagine the story behind the picture. Students produce the new version. Some ideas for re-creation media are: a "radio play", recorded on tape; a written short story; a story in comic strip form.; a narrative poem; a painting; a display for the classroom.

11. Co-operative Learning

In cooperative learning strategy, students work togetherto achieve a particular goal. To facilitate the cooperative learning, individual accountability, face to face interaction, interpersonal and social skills, positive interdependence and group processing are essential.

The Jigsaw method (Aronson, 1978) is one of the cooperative learning method that can be effectively used in Human Rights education. A model lesson for teaching human Rights by Jigsaw method is given below:

12. Case Study Method

A case study is an in depth study of a problem. It focuses on a single case / incident /occurrence rather than on extended events. The method provide active participation of students and develop critical thinking in them. Also it develops citizenship skills.

Procedure: Choose a case and define the case. An identifiable problem situation should be inherent in the case which stimulates the student to think. The case should raise important questions for the student to solve. Critically examine the case and arrive at conclusion based on facts. The findings may be generalized.

MODEL LESSONS

UNIVERSAL DECLARATION OF HUMAN RIGHTS

(By the Method of Jigsaw)

(*Source*: Human Rights Educators' Network)

Time: 60–5 minutes

Topic: Universal declaration of human Rights

Objectives of the Lesson: The lesson has the following objectives

1. To recognize abuses and affirmations of all of the articles of the UDHR.
2. To learn about typical rights situations in specific countries.
3. To work collaboratively and effectively with peers

Procedure: Give each student a copy of the UDHR and selected Newspaper cuttings reported Human rights violations.

Divide students into groups of 3-5. Each of these 'research groups' is assigned a different set of 3-6 sentences from different newspaper cuttings.

For example, Group A takes sentences 1-6 sentences from cutting No-1, Group B sentences 7-12 from cutting no-2, and so on.

The research groups take 15-20 minutes to find 2 or more articles from the UDHR that apply to each sentence. For example,, ' The Palestinian Problem.'

This indicates an abuse of Article 3 (right to life) and the Indigenous People's rights. Each student makes his or her own list of articles based on the research group discussion. A guided practice as a whole class may be necessary.

Students are now put into 'home groups' as follows. If there are 4 students in each research group, number the students 1-4. The 'ones' get together as Home Group 1, all the 'twos' form Home Group 2, and so on.

Once in home groups, the students report the findings of their research group. For instance, in Home Group 1, there should be one student from Research Group A, one from Research Group B, and so on. The representative from Research Group A reports on sentences 1-6, etc.

At the end of reporting, each student should write UDHR article numbers related to each case in the paper cutting (30-45 minutes).

Discuss selected sentences as a whole class to check for understanding and pursue areas that interest the students. (at least 10 minutes)

Some of the cases which can be used as paper cuttings are listed below:

1. Palestinians demonstrate for statehood.
2. The Chinese government punishes a couple for having a second child.
3. The government of Turkey burns down villages of Kurds—a people of southeast Turkey— and forces them to go to new towns.
4. A Brazilian child is denied a school education because the family can't afford it.
5. A criminal in El Salvador is held in jail for months without being charged with any crime.
6. A woman in India is forced to marry a man whom she does not want to marry.
7. Students in the Philippines gather to discuss current issues.
8. Attack on World Trade Centre in America on 11th September 2001.
9. Students in Germany regularly read the newspaper about politics in their country and human rights in other countries.
10. Parents of children with birth defects in the area of Chernobyl demand information from the Russian government on the effects of a nuclear accident.
11. A teacher insults a student and punish him for incorrectly answering a question.
12. Students in the U.S. and Canada write letters to Pakistan and India to end forced child labour.

II) MODEL NO. 2

Topic: Right For Balanced Food

Class:- VI	**Subject: Science**

Curriculum Statement:- Students get awareness regarding the importance of balanced food for a healthy living.

Requirement:

Activities

Evaluation

Teacher presents the photos of two children.One of them having malnourishment & the Other normal health — using OHP.	Class quizzes
Following by the general discussion in the class	Class test.Group level evaluation

Discussion points **What is the main distinguishing feature of the First baby from the second? Peer evaluation**

What are the reasons for their differences in their health?

Can you suggest ways to improve the condition of the first baby?

Discussion follows- Teachers adds more points- and concludes the discussion.

Teacher divides the class into 5 groups and assigned them a task of reading material (health through the healthy food) from the health magazine (say eg: Mathrubhumi health magazine), followed by certain questions.

Students read the material and discuss the answers and note the points.

Group presentation – while one group presents others add more points.

Hence students get awareness regarding the need for healthy food and having it for their daily life.

News covering in- different news papers – for health.

Group activity- papers to each group- group goes the news papers and finds the weightage given to the news in a particular news paper- regarding the health with another news daily.

Students cut particular news/features/photos, etc. and prepares health wall magazine and exhibits them.

Group evaluate others work- teacher congratulates and suggest ways to improve their works.

Assignment: Group activity- News coverage in T V for health and healthy living – a survey.

III) MODEL NO. 3

Topic: Right to Live.

Class: VI **Subject: Science**

CS: To collect information in conservation of water, pollution control. Need for the controlled consumption of the water.

Requirements:

Activities. **Evaluation**

Teacher presents a news from a news daily – regarding the Hospitalization of some people after drinking polluted water.

News.

____

____

____

· One student reads it loudly,

· Followed by the general discussion-regarding the probable causes for the water pollution.

· Teacher divides them in to 6 groups and each group takes a lot, which contain a problem to investigate by them.

· Students sit in respective group and plan the action and prepares the necessary Questionnaire for the survey.

Each group presents their survey design and through the discussion improve it.

Conduct of the Survey: Collect the data, and water samples from different places and analyses for determining the amount of pollutants.

Prepares the report.

Present the report through Seminar.

Followed by discussion and conclusion.

Conclusion: Pollution, pollutants, the causes and Human activities leading to pollution.. need for the water conservation and controlled usage, etc. are to be discussed and pupils made aware of importance of water in their life as a life saving substance.

Assignments: Find out the different life threatening activities around you, especially by polluting other resources-like water. Collects the necessary materials as evidence and exhibits them.Prepare the report.

IMPLEMENTATION OF HUMAN RIGHTS EDUCATION

The introduction of human rights education in schools and colleges in recent years is a progressive step and the various bodies involved in evolving a programme for human rights education deserve to be commended. However, what is discouraging to note is that the subject is taught as an academic discipline. When the subject becomes an academic discipline students learn the subject like any other. In the process, passing an examination by memorizing notes becomes more important than a commitment to the victims of human rights through a dialogue with them and fighting against the violators of human rights.

When the whole issue of human rights education was being debated and was proposed by the National Human Rights Commission (NHRC) that it is to be incorporated in the syllabus as a separate subject in schools and universities, the then Chairman of the National Human Rights Commission, Justice Ranganath Mishra went far as to say that it should be taught all the way from primary school to the highest level of university. There arises the chance for two types of pedagogy in human Rights education.One pedagogy basically thinks of transmitting the knowledge and thinking on human rights developed in middle class circles among what are called educationists in organizations like the NCERT and such other arenas of well intentioned and well motivated desire to transmit human rights thinking among the young and not so young through curricula development, through encouragement of research in these areas, and instruments of pedagogic transmission that is available to those in charge of modern education.

There is another pedagogy, which is also emerging in our own country as well as others like us. That draws upon what is going on in society and among the people. A pedagogy, that struggles against hegemony, and for due regard and dignity for human beings, and to structure the research, the teaching and even the training and curricula development, to use the cliché 'education from the bottom up'. It is not until, that the former pedagogy draws more and more from the knowledge, insights and wisdom of the latter, including some sorbid realities, and some not so pleasant realities, thrown up by the experience of the latter, that genuine enlightenment on human rights and related matters would take place.

Rights are involved in major struggles for rights, establishment of rights all the way from the theory of natural rights to what, in recent years, is called human rights, following the United Nations Declaration on Human Rights, rights have involved major upheavals – social, cultural, political and economic and to an extent even spiritual.

We are already engrossed in a rather authoritarian culture. For a central body, emerging from that authoritarian culture, to impose a syllabus on the school system or the college and university system would be a wrong approach. There can be no education on human rights through school and college curriculum. Many years ago, under the auspices of the UNESCO, an attempt was made to engage educationists in India in human rights education.

Education on human rights is not to be achieved through syllabi or curricula drafted in ivory towers, for that matter, even by research bodies, research centres that claim to be in touch with basic local realities. Human rights can best be experienced personally and in becoming and in the context of community and what a community is striving for.

Education in human rights has to be addressed to those who are perpetrators of human rights violation. And those who are at the receiving end bear suffering patiently; they must be supported. Human rights and violations of human rights are to be found in that school of life, not in schools located,

We have to remember something that Dr. Pal has mentioned but doesn't develop sufficiently. The development on human rights in a plural and highly diverse society and, highly diverse polity.

There has been a great deal of talk following Kargil that both India and the United States are democracies and, therefore, attempt should be made for a collaboration between these two countries. Mrs. Madeleine Albright, Secretary of State, the United States of America on one hand and Mr. Jaswant Singh, India's Former External Affairs Minister on the other have fully agreed and indeed he deputed a government official to go and discuss in Washington the possibility of greater collaboration between these two countries. But the democracy as understood in the United States and democracy as understood by ourselves over the national independence movement, over the assertions of the integral pluralism of Indian society, are not identical.In other words, we took to democracy not because of the fascination of an imported model but because of our own compulsion and above all our own interest, our desire for preserving our pluralism and our great diversity.

On the other hand, the larger system is helping to perpetuate inequality, poverty, disparities; it is becoming an instrument of globalisation, ignoring the pressures that are emanating from below, the pressure for justice, the pressure for equity, the pressure for rewarding the oppressed sections of society; in short, the deprived and oppressed are making a determined demand for a chance in life.

So we are caught in between these two thrusts, the thrust of globalisation on the one hand and of an upsurge of democratic aspirations from the bottom on the other. The system that we have, the system that we grafted on an authoritarian political culture and drew sustenance from that authoritarian political culture with its feudal and big business and export house backing, is the system through which we propose to educate our young in human rights. It is an impossible undertaking. It is an undertaking that is fraught with enormous risks and particularly risks to those who are craving more than any other section of society to use the instrumentalities of democracy for achieving their goals in life and livelihoods that they crave for.

Human rights is not something to be exported from one country to other countries, nor is it something to be resisted just because it is being exported. Human rights is valued because people value it, valued because people struggle around this issue, valued because it is through the achievement of rights that it will be possible to deal with the turbulences, the upsurges, the convulsions, and for this we have to focus our work and research and everything else into the social arena. We have to make life the school of human rights rather than schools, colleges and universities, the school for human rights.

University Grants Commission takes the initiative for promoting human rights education in universities and institutions of higher learning. One would have been happier if the issue was kept open and was decided through a wide-ranging discussion among teachers at all levels of the educational set-up. If the decision were reached through the process of such discussions, the rationale for introducing it at a particular level would have been clarified. As no wide-ranging discussions were organized, we are completely in the dark as to why human rights education should begin with higher education and not earlier.

Human rights are about the rights of others that we should respect as much as about rights that we ourselves claim. If we grow up with the conviction and belief that our rights of others, such a belief can be difficult and hard to break or change in later life. This being the case, it would seem that human rights education should begin as early in life as possible. If it is introduced at later stages of the education process, the chances are that by the time a child gets these his or her attitudes would have already hardened so much that they would be almost impossible to change. The case for the introduction of human rights education at an early stage of the educative process thus seems strong.

Those opposed to the introduction of human rights education early in life often invoke the argument that human rights are too abstract a concept to be introduced too early in the education of a child. Frankly, this is too facile an argument and does not make sense. If a child can be introduced to the intricacies of plant life, human organism or the universe (whose teaching begins in our schools at an early age), one fails to see why human rights education should necessarily be postponed until later. It is not as if abstract things cannot be taught to a child at lower levels of educational process. It simply means that they ought to be taught at a less sophisticated level of abstraction than would be possible at higher levels. Thus, the argument that human rights education is too abstract a subject and a student would not grasp it if he or she is exposed to it too early in life does not seem entirely tenable either in terms of educational theory or current practices in educational curricula.

Purely from the perspective of efficacy and practical relevance, human rights education ought to begin as early as possible in schools. Ideally, if it were possible to educate parents through modern communication technologies to take on the responsibility of creating sense of human rights among their children, human rights education should begin in the home itself. Since this does not seem possible in the foreseeable future, all the more in a national environment where the thrust is towards denial of human rights, human rights education should begin early at school.

Closely linked to this is another issue. It is whether human rights should be taught as part of the curriculum or as a distinct subject. On this question again a clear position does not seem to emerge from current discourse and academic practice has a tendency to be remarkably confused. The University Grants Commission issued a circular to university Vice-chancellors soliciting responses and proposals as to how human rights education might be developed. The Vice-chancellors in turn referred the circular to different faculties in their universities. The general opinion expressed by the faculty members at such discussions was that human rights education should be built into the teaching programmes of the different disciplines rather than be introduced as a subject of study and research in itself. No further discussion took place thereafter on how this was to be done. In other words, how the different disciplines were to be sensitized to human rights was left open.

The University Grants Commission sanctioned liberal grants to university departments and colleges, already starved of funds for academic engagement, to hold seminars on human rights to which only the initiated were in any case to be (and were actually) invited as well as decided to set up separate units for the study of human rights. In other words, the decision on this issue again seems to have been taken without any conclusive discussion as to whether human rights education would constitute a part of the general programme of teaching of disciplines or would be promoted as a separate area of teaching and research.

This brings the question of an appropriate pedagogy for human rights education. Should it be taught routinely to generate familiarity with the concept of human rights? Or, should it be used as a means of promoting a revolutionary consciousness so that those having been exposed to that education become active agents for the struggle for human rights. Anyone who has been a part of the teaching process at any level will easily admit that even a potentially positive subject like human rights can be taught in a most routine manner so that it would eventually entail communication of the concept of human rights without contributing to the growth of a critical consciousness. It is possible to design a curriculum for human rights education in a manner that information on what are human rights and how they developed is imparted without making the recipient capable of relating human rights to his or her own daily experience in concrete situations.

One of the great tragedies of the contemporary Indian situation is that a relatively small number of children are able to go into channel of formal education and even smaller numbers go in for higher education. Under the circumstances, if the base of human rights education has to be broadened, then it cannot be limited to institutions of formal learning. It would have to be extended to include those (and they constitute a huge number) who are at present not listed for formal education at all. In the strategy of human rights education this population does not figure at all.. It appears that the current strategy of human rights education, quite apart from the other weaknesses to which attention has been drawn earlier, ought to be reoriented to address this large population as well.

Based on the discussions which the present book is dealt with and taking the model lesson included here as models, the author conducted a series of workshops among experts in the field for incorporating human rights education in the existing Secondary School Curriculum of Kerala State with the assistance of University Grants Commission.

The attempt was successful and the products of the workshops are given in next chapter.

REFERENCES

1. Vijapur, A.P.& Suresh. K. (1999), *Perspectives on Human Rights,* New Delhi: Manak Publications.
2. Tarrow, N. B. (1987), *Human Rights and Education*, England: Pergamon Press.
3. *The Protection of Human Rights Act, 1993 with Kerala Rules*, (1998), Cochin: Suvarna Publications.
4. Mohanty, J., *Human Rights Education*, New Delhi: Deep& Deep Publications.
5. Pal, R.M. & Chakraborthy, S. (2000), *Human Rights Education in India*.
6. Council of Europe (1981), *The teaching of human rights*. Report on the Eighth European Seminar of teachers in Member states. Donaueschingen. Federal Republic of Germany, May 19-23, 1980.
7. Churchill, S. & Omari, I. (1981), Evaluation of UNESCO Associated schools Project in education for international cooperation and peace. (ERIC Documentation Reproduction service. No. ED 110214).
8. UNESCO (1978), *Proceedings of the International Congress on Teaching of Human Rights*. Vienna.:UNESCO.
9. UNESCO (1982), *Experts meeting on the teaching of human rights.* (UNESCO Document No. SS-82/Conf.401/24). Strasbourg: International Institute of Human rights.

10. UNESCO (1983), *Synthesis of member states reports on the application of the recommendation concerning education for international understanding, cooperation and peace and education relating to human rights and fundamental freedoms.* (UNESCO Document ED 83/ Conf. 214/2).
11. Raman, K.S.(2000), Human Rights Education: Pedagogy and empowerment problems and prospects. *Journal of Institute of Human Rights.*
12. Flowers, N. (1989), *Human Rights Here and Now.* Minneapolis, MN. Human Rights Educator's Network
13. Teaching Human Rights, (1988), New York: United Nations, 1989.
14. Bhattacharya, G.C. (2001), Teaching Human Rights at the B.Ed level;Needs and Objectives. *University News,*Vol 39, No.52
15. Singh, A. (2001), Human Rights: Need for Sensitising the learner. *University News,*Vol 39, No.52.
16. Pike, G. & Selby, D. (1990), *Human Rights :an activity File.* U.K.: Stanley Thorns publishers.
17. Panda, P. (2006), Human Rights Education in Schools Perspectives and challenges. *Journal of Indian Education*
18. *Human Rights Education,* (1996), Self Learning Module for Teacher Educators. New Delhi: N.C.T.E.
19. Subramanian, S. (1997), *Human Rights–International Challenges.* New Delhi: Institute of World Congress on Human Rights.
20. Dhand, H. (2000), *Teaching Human Rights; A Hand book for teacher Educators.* Bhopal: Asian Institute of Human Rights Education.
21. Rajagopal, B. (2000), The Supreme Court and Human Rights. *The Hindu*, 6 December.
22. Amnesty International Human Rights Education Network.

4

Human Rights Education in Practice
(Model Lessons)

MODEL LESSONS ENGLISH FOR STANDARDS VIII, IX and X

Standard VIII

ENGLISH

UNIT I—The boy who broke the bank.

Curriculum Objectives

- Express ideas and attends debates and discussions.
- Prepares questions based on a topic.
- Prepares posters based on a topic.

Human Rights

- Right to Education
- Right against exploitation

➤ **Let us debate**

Teacher puts forward a statement, "Nathu is solely responsible for the breakdown of the Pipal Nagar Bank". The students are asked to share their opinion.

Arguments for Nathu	**Arguments against Nathu**
He is illiterate	He said he is not paid
He is unaware of the State of Bank	....
....	....

➤ Let us prepare a questionnaire

Nathu is waiting on the steps of the Pipal Nagar Bank expecting Seth Govind Ram. Suppose you are a journalist. Prepare a questionnaire to seek information about the breakdown of the bank and his role in it.

➤ Group discussion

Nathu's illiteracy resulted in the breakdown of the Pipal Nagar Bank. What are the disadvantages of illiteracy. Let the students list out.

➤ Prepare a Poster

Literacy helps the nation. Let the pupils prepare some slogans highlighting the importance of literacy in the Society.

Standard IX

ENGLISH

UNIT III —The Pledge of INA

Curriculum Objectives

- Reads the article and comprehends it
- Infers and understands the intended meaning of a discourse
- Narrates events and experiences
- Participates in discussions
- Prepares questionnaire to conduct an interview
- Learns to write short notes

Human Rights

- Right to Nationality
- Right to liberty and security
- Right to self determination

Activities

➤ **General Discussion**

On the last Presidential election in India—Candidates - A.P.J.Abdul Kalam and Captain Lakshmi - Capt. Lakshmi - a living legend —leaders of women wing of INA.

➤ **Shall we frame some questions?**

Pupils sit in groups of five and prepare maximum number of questions to conduct an interview with Captain Lakshmi.

Questions:

Madam, you are the most famous person who was related to INA and is still living. Can you explain how you got contact with INA and Netaji ?

How old were you at that time ?

What was your work in INA ?

How do you feel now about the relation with Netaji and as the Captain of women wing of INA ?

....

FREEDOM MY BIRTH RIGHT

➤ **Let's Compare**

Some features of dependent India and Indepedent India are given. Let them complete the table provided.

Dependent India	**Independent India**
Depends British in all fields	Independent in all fields
In Education	Political freedom
Job Opportunity	Equal justice
....	Equal Opportunity
....	....

➤ **Let's Collect**

Pupils are asked to collect the pictures of freedom fighters and make notes on their contribution towards upholding of liberty, self determination and national spirit.

Eg: Mahatma Gandhi—Struggled against discrimination

Standard X

ENGLISH

UNIT II—Two Gentlemen of Verona

Curriculum Objectives

- Reads the article and comprehends it
- Infers and understands the intended meaning
- Prepares Questions on a given passage

Human Rights Contents Specifications

- Right to Life
- Right to Shelter
- Right to Food
- Right to Security

Activities

Teacher exhibits a documentary on war in the class. Discussion follows on the after effects of War.

➤ **Let's List**

Comforts and conveniences they enjoy at home. Different groups list out the comforts and conveniences they enjoy.

Eg: (a) Food (b) Shelter (c) Security.....

➤ **Shall we frame some questions?**

Pupil read paragraphs 19 to 21 of Unit 2 (individual) Sit in group of 5 and prepare maximum number of questions based on passage followed by question answer session.

➤ **WAR!WAR!WAR!**

Do Nicola and Jacopa enjoy the facilities enjoyed by you?

What facilities are denied to them?

Pupil sit in groups and list out maximum number of after effect of war.

- Loss of Shelter

- Loss of Security
- Starvation

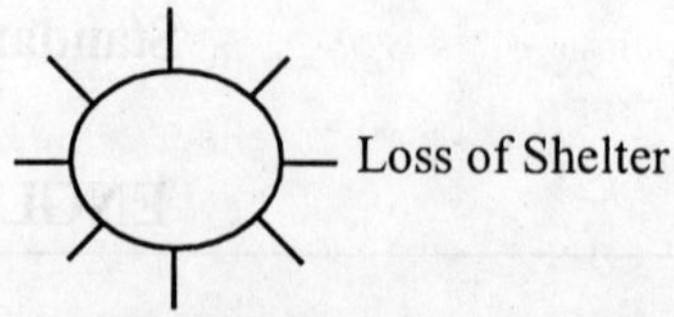

➤ **Let's Compare**

Pupil	Characters
1. Get Shelter	1. Lost Shelter
2.	2. ....
3.	3. ....
4	4 ....
5	5 ....

Discussion

Why were the characters denied the facilities?

➤ **Dont's Deny Our Rights**

Teacher distributes copies of reading materials (UDHR documents) to the groups

Pupil list out the rights which were denied to war victims.

➤ **War & Peace**

Pupil collect pictures of war related problems and give captions.

MODEL LESSONS HINDI FOR STANDARDS VIII, IX and X

VIII th Standard

Topic : **कलम का सिपाही।**
Human Right : Right to Freedom of expression (1948-UDHR-Article 19)
Curricular Objectives : स्वतंत्रतापूर्ण आशयाभिव्यक्ति से संबंधित जीवनी पढ़कर समझना।
Requirements : महात्माओं की जीवनी जिसमें स्वतंत्र रूप से आशयाभिव्यक्ति हो। लेख/कविता जिस में भी स्वतंत्र रूप से आशयाभिव्यक्ति हो।
Grouping : पाँच-पाँच सदस्यों के दस ग्रुप।
Activities : स्वतंत्रतापूर्ण आशयाभिव्यक्ति से युक्त

- कविताएँ, नाटक, जीवनी, आत्मकथा आदि लाने का निर्देश दें।
- साहित्यिक विधा के आधार पर ग्रुप अपनाएँ।
- हर एक ग्रुप अपनी-अपनी साहित्यिक विधा में प्रतिपादित स्वतंत्रता पूर्ण आशयाभिव्यक्ति पर चर्चा करें।
- हर एक ग्रुप अपनी-अपनी राय प्रस्तुत करें।
- ग्रुपों के बीच में चर्चा और शंका समाधान।
- स्वतंत्रतापूर्ण आशयाभिव्यक्ति के विरुद्ध अखबारों में आए समाचारों का संकलन।
- कक्षा में उनकी प्रस्तुती और चर्चा।
- चर्चा के उपरांत छात्र इस निष्कर्ष पर पहुँचता है कि अब भी हमारे समाज में इसी प्रकार की घटनाएँ होती हैं। उनको हमारे समाज से दूर करना हमारा कर्तव्य है।

Seminar : स्वतंत्रतापूर्ण आशयाभिव्यक्ति चाहिए या नहीं। विषय पर संगोष्ठि चलाएँ।

Exhibition : स्वतंत्रतापूर्ण आशयाभिव्यक्ति के विरुद्ध अखबारों में आए समाचार तथा चित्र इकट्ठा करें तथा कक्षा में एक प्रदर्शनी चलाएँ।

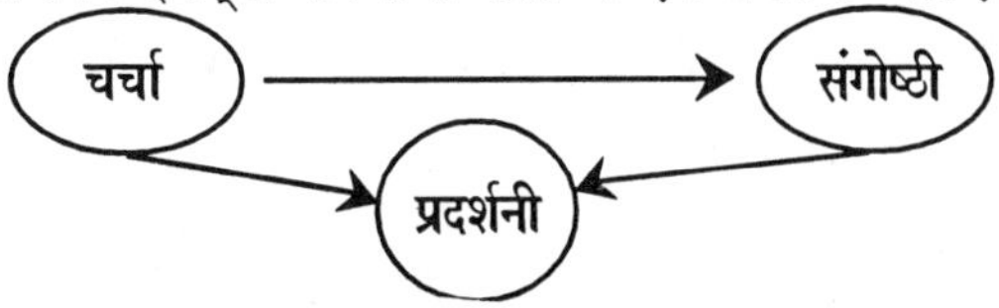

Standard IX

Topic : **गिल्लू।**

Human Right : Right to life

Curricular Objectives : जीने के अधिकार से संबंधित रेखाचित्र पढ़कर आशयग्रहण।

Requirements

- जीने के अधिकार के संबंध में अखबारों में आए समाचार और लेख। जीने के अधिकार के विरुद्ध समाचार।
- जीने के अधिकार और उसके विरुद्ध घटनाएँ तथा तत्संबंधी चित्र।
- प्रश्नावली जिसमें जीने के अधिकार से संबंधित प्रश्न हो।

Activities

- जीने के अधिकार के संबंध में अखबारों में आए समाचार तथा लेख इकट्ठा करें।
- ग्रुप में चर्चा करके प्रस्तुत करें।
- जीने के अधिकार के विरुद्ध समाचार पर भी चर्चा करें।
- धारणाओं का प्रस्तुतीकरण।
- उसके संबंध में प्रश्नोत्तरी।
- जीने के अधिकार के विरुद्ध हमारे समाज में अपने गाँव में क्या क्या धारणाएँ होती हैं?

  इसकी एक पैमाइश (Survey) करने के लिए छात्र प्रश्नावली तैयार करें।
- कक्षा में चर्चा करके अंतिम रूप दें।
- अपने गाँव में पैमाइश (Survey) चलाएँ।

Standard X

Topic : **अनमोल यादें।**

Human Right : Right to Non-Discrimination.

Curricular Objectives : किसी महान व्यक्ति के जीवन संबंधी विवेचन की घटना पर आधारित आत्म कथांश सुन पढ़कर समझना।

Requirements

- विवेचन संबंधी समाचार जो दैनिक समाचार-पत्रों में आए हो।
- विवेचन संबंधी तस्वीर।
- जीवनी जिसमें विवेचन संबंधी घटनाएँ हो।

Activities

अब्दुल कलाम की जीवन संबंधी घटना को ध्यान में रखकर अन्य महान व्यक्तियों के जीवन में घटित विवेचन संबंधी घटनाओं का संकलन करके अगले दिन इनका निर्देश अध्यापिका दें।

Grouping

पाँच-पाँच सदस्यों को दस ग्रुप।

- छात्रों द्वारा लाए विवेचन संबंधी सामग्री पर हर एक ग्रुप में चर्चा।
- उसके बाद अध्यापिका लाए विवेचन संबंधी सामग्री ग्रुप में बाँटना तथा उसके बारे में भी चर्चा।
- हर एक ग्रुप विवेचन पर जाँच करना तथा उसको समझना।
- इन निष्कर्षों की अब्दुल कलाम के जीवन विवेचन से तुलना करना।
- आज की परिस्थितियों से तुलना करना तथा विश्लेषण करना।
- तब इस निष्कर्ष पर पहुँचना कि विवेचन बिताना हमारा अधिकार है।

Assignments

- समाचार पत्रों में आए विवेचन संबंधी समाचारों का संकलन करना।
- विवेचन के हेतुओं को तैयार करना। (ग्रुप कार्य)

Seminar

विवेचन रहित समाज–कल, आज और कल।

अध्यापिका लाए सामग्री

- जब गाँधीजी दक्षिण अफ्रीका में रेलगाड़ी पर यात्रा कर रहे थे उस समय एक अंग्रेज अफसर ने उनको रेलगाड़ी से बाहर ढकेल दिया।
- डॉ. अम्बेदकर हर दिन एक बोरी (टाट) लेकर स्कूल जाते थे। क्योंकि बेंच सिर्फ ऊँची जाति के छात्रों को देते थे। अम्बेदकर कक्षा के एक कोने में बोरा बिछाकर बैठते थे।

MODEL LESSONS IN OTHER SUBJECTS

SOCIAL SCIENCE

Standard VIII **Unit VII**

THE CULTURAL PAST (KERALA)

Sub Units: Caste System, "Devadasi" System, Landlordism, Feudal System and Matriarchy

Curriculum Objectives

- To collect details about the Caste system and its adverse effects on Kerala society from various sources.
- To collect more data from different sources about the activities done in Kerala against the caste system.
- To evaluate the rise and fall of the Devadasi system
- To collect the details about how the Landlordism and the feudal system affected the ownership of Land and misery of serfs.
- To collect and analyse the features of land reforms from various books, news papers and other medias.
- To evaluate the features of Matriarchy and its causes of destructions.

➤ **Human Rights**

- Right to non discrimination
- Right to women

➤ **Teaching Learning materials required**

1. *Kerala Samskaram*, A. Sreedhara Menon
2. *Kerala Samskara Charithram*, Dr. V.K. Gopalakrishnan
3. *Kerala Charithrathinte Irulandanja Edukal*, Elamkulam Kunhanpillai.

Expected time : 4 periods

Process	Response
Let learners note down the existing bad customs individually. Share it in 3 member group. Presentation—discussion Discussion Points: Why don't we see the old customs today? Then, Teacher presents a topic for Seminar. Are you aware of the social conditions in the past? Teacher assigns the group to prepare a separate seminar paper on the following sub areas: Group A— Caste System B— Devadasi System C— Land Lordism/Feudal System D— Matriarchy Students prepare the seminar paper separately in groups. Students are given the reference books and teacher ensures the assistance as and when required. Each group prepares a seminar paper and plan for the presentation. **Seminar Presentation** Selection of Moderator—Moderator explains the purpose of seminar and gives instructions for each group. Group A — Seminar paper presentation Group B — Seminar paper presentation Group C — Seminar paper presentation Group D — Seminar paper presentation Let each group present their opinions, ideas and doubts. Teacher facilitates as and when required. Consolidation by Moderator. Consolidation by facilitator. **Preparation of Seminar Report.** Let all prepare a report on Seminar. Teacher explains the structure of seminar report. **Assignments** Assign them to prepare a write up on the following a) Land Lordism b) Devadasi System c) Matriarchy d) Caste system	

Standard IX **Unit II**

AREAS OF COMMERCE

Curriculum Objectives

☞ To understand the concepts regarding sales, policy of buying, marketing, rights of consumers and sellers by participating discussion and writing short notes.

Human rights

Right to liberty and security

Right to freedom of expression

Right to self determination

Expected time : 2 periods

Discussion on

Best producer/Best consumer

A good consumer or best producer which one you prefer to become?

Elicits the answers

To seek more details regarding rights of consumer—Teacher arranges an Interaction with a Lawyer.

Groups are formed to prepare questions for interview/interaction.

Presentation of interview schedule—

Discussion & modification

Conduct of Interview/interaction

Teacher asks to write report on Interview (Assignment)

Standard IX **Unit IV**

EUROPE TOWARDS MODERNISM

Curriculum Objectives

- ☞ To collect details from various sources about factors led to renaissance and to formulate opinions.
- ☞ To understand the changes created by humanism in Modern European society and know the need of humanism.
- ☞ To formulate concepts about the changes created by literature, science and art in renaissance.
- ☞ To collect details about scientists, artists, writers in renaissance period.

Human rights

Right to life

Right to self determination

Prohibition of torture and of cruel inhuman or degrading treatment or punishment.

Right to freedom of thought, conscience and religion

Right to freedom of expression

Teaching Learning materials required

History of World Civilization (selected portion)

World History (Vol 2)

Prof. E.Sreedhar, K.P.Devadas (selected portion)

Expected time—six periods

Teacher presents unforgettable events from the life of Galileo, Coppernicus (Fought against the then government)

Discussion—Renaissance and scientists—discussion should be focussed on renaissance matters.

Seminar

Topic: The impact of Renaissance in various fields.

Teacher divides the class in 4 different groups and assign the sub topics to each group.

Group A — Changes in Literature

B — Science & Renaissance

C — Religion & Renaissance

D — Growth and changes in Art.

Each group prepares seminar paper separately.

Teacher facilitates each group by providing necessary reading materials, and hints.

Presentation of Seminar papers.

Selects a Moderator

Moderator explains the instructions.

Group A — Presents the seminar paper

Group B — " "

Group C — " "

Group D — " "

Let each group members raise their doubts and opinions

Teacher facilitates

After the consodilation by moderator teacher concludes the seminar session.

Seminar Report Writing

Teacher asks to write seminar report individually (Assignment)

Teacher reminds them—structure of a good seminar report.

Next day—saminar report presentation (Random)

Assignment

To what extend the freedom utilized (right to expression, right to question) by scientists in renaissance period?

Write a short note on 'Bruno', Galileo, Coppornicus.

By discussion, reference students are directed to complete the assignments.

Presentation and Discussion

Consolidation by Teacher

Making Bullettin Board

Teacher asks students to collect picture, photos of Galileo, Coppornicus and Bruno and prepare a short profile of them.

Standard IX **Unit II**

THE ATMOSPHERE OF THE EARTH

Curriculum Objectives

- To collect information using observations, reading materials about the relationship between the man and the atmosphere, to arrive a conclusion about the impact of various strata of atmosphere on the living organisms, how it affects the environment, and to understand the need for the protection of the environment and encourage to involve various activities to protect the environment.
- To collect details and make conclusion about the temperature of atmosphere.
- To find out the relation between atmospheric pressure and temperature and how it influences weather using information from surroundings and reading materials.
- To understand more about the extent of exploitation of natural resources, need of preservation of resources by using reading materials and participating in disucssions.
- To build positive attitude towards the protection of resources.

Human Rights

Right to environment

Right to life

Right to enjoy the highest standards of physical and mental health.

Teaching Learning materials required

CD ROMs—related to TSUNAMI and Global Warming, News paper reports photos, pictures.

Expected time: 6 periods

Activity 1

Seminar

Topic "**Global Environment**" What and How?

In the beginning

Share the information about Tsunami based on pictures, and newspaper reports.

Following this—Teacher shows CDs related to the topic.

Global Warming

Ozone Depletion

Ozone layer

Increase of Chlorofluro carbon

Rise of sea level

After the CD show

Teacher facilitates a short discussion

Teacher divides the class into groups.

Each group prepares seminar paper on sub topic given above.

Teacher render assistance to each group by providing reading materials.

Select moderator

Conducts seminar paper presentation- Let pupil clear their doubts and express opinions- Teacher concludes the seminar session.

Teacher asks to write Seminar Report **(Assignment)**

Presentation of Seminar Report.

Standard X **Unit XIII**

HUMAN RIGHTS

Curriculum Objectives

- ☞ To collect details from various sources about Human rights and define what is meant by human right and present them through discussion, debates.
- ☞ To collect information and prepare a special edition about UN Charter, Declaration of Human rights, efforts to protect human rights using CD ROMs, reading materials.

Human rights

UDHR Articles

Human rights guaranteed in International treaties.

Teaching Learning Materials required

News paper cuttings, Newspaper reports, periodicals

Expected time : 2 periods

Teacher presents pictures and cases related to the violation of human rights.

Discussion

Teacher ask the students to prepare a short note on

"Human Rights".

For this, the class is divided into groups

Teacher provides necessary reading materials to each group.

Students write short note individually and share it in pair group.

Presentation (random)

Discussion

Teacher consolidate the discussion

Group discussion on

Content of UN Charter

Preparation of Special Edition on

"HUMAN RIGHTS"

Teacher asks to each group to prepare a magazine on Human right.

Teacher facilitate in each group.

Releasing of the prepared Magazine in School Assembly

Standard X **Unit XIII**

HUMAN RIGHTS (*Continued*)

Curriculum Objectives

- ☞ To collect the information from various sources about efforts done for protecting Human rights by Indian Constitution, National Human right Commission.
- ☞ To collect information from News paper and media about the activities of State, National Commission of Human rights and present it in a different mode.

Human Rights

UDHR Articles

Human rights guaranteed in International treaties.

Expected Time : 2 periods

Discussion

Teacher presents a new item published on December 10—Teacher initiates a short discussion on the item read.

Hints: Teacher provides each group

1) Extractsof Human Rights, Declaration of 1948

2) Extract of Indian Constitution articles related to human rights

Consolidation by teacher- Teacher seeks attention on—A newspaper report "The weight of School Bag"

(State human right commission has taken the matter as human right violation)—Whole discussion on the news report

Preparation of Bulletin Board.

Teacher askes the students to collect pictures, photo, and other detials of State and National Human right commission and exhibit in a Bulletin Board. Displaying of the bulletin board in the school Notice Board.

Standard X **Unit XIII**

HUMAN RIGHTS (*Continued*)

Curriculum Objectives

- ☞ To collect details from various sources about the concepts like law, freedom, equity and formulate ideas such as equality, justice, law, literacy and present these through discussions, short notes.
- ☞ To evaluate, analyse and collect details from various sources about the violation of human rights in national and international level towards children, women, dalits, persons in police custody.

Human rights

UDHR Articles

Human rights guaranteed in International treaties.

Teaching Learning Materials required

News paper cuttings, Newspaper reports, periodicals

Expected time : 2 periods

Interview 1

Teacher divides the class into groups and ask them to prepare questions for interview with a ***lawyer***.

Conducts Interview

Report writing on Interview

Interview 2

Teacher shows a news item related to Police custody death—Discussion, conducts an interview with Police Officer. Asks them to write short note on Interview.

Standard X **Unit XIII**

HUMAN RIGHTS (*Continued*)

Curriculum Objectives

☞ To collect details and arrive a conclusion about the role of NGOs in protecting human rights.

Human Rights

UDHR Articles

Human rights guaranteed in International treaties.

Teaching Learning Materials required

Expected time 8 periods

Prepare a report on activities of human right done by NGO during the past 3 months.

Teacher divides the class into groups

Each group examines the report, analyse it and prepare a report.

Teacher render the help in each group

Presentation of report

Discussion

Consolidation by Teacher

Project

To what extend the violation of human rights happens today?

Planning for project

Students decides the methodology of study with the help of teacher.

Let them discuss in groups about note of NGO's

Data collection

Referring modes

Interview with lawyer, journalists, Historian.

Teacher provides each group necessary reading materials.

Teacher ask the students to prepare questions for interview.

Group work

Presentation—refinement.

Prepare general questionnaire with the help of Teacher.

Conducts Interview

Presentatin of findings before the class by groups.

Data consolidation by each group

Let them complete the project

Report writing

Presentation of Project Report.

Seminar

Topic "*Violation of Human rights and protection of Law*"

Each group presents the findings of the project they conducted, through seminar—

Report writing

Teacher asks each student to write a report on seminar conducted.

Collect pictures, related to violation of Human rights and ask them to display in school notice board.

BIOLOGY

Standard VIII

TOPIC: AGRICULTURE IN KERALA

Curriculum Objectives

Through field trips, Interview, Secondary data analysis—to recognize the importance of agriculture in the development of various fields of production.

To sensitize the need for adopting the most appropriate seeds and techniques in accordance with the geographical and climatic features of Kerala.

Human rights : 1. Right for healthy living

2. Right for the protection of environment.

ACTIVITIES

What and Why?

Teacher and the students together sing the following song:

....

....

(SONG related to agriculture)

Followed by discussion on

— **Various types of Agriculture in Kerala**

— **Teacher concludes.**

Group Discussion

Teacher divides students into 5 groups and provide a reading material on our old ways of agriculture.

Students discuss on it

Present their views

Teacher concludes

Teacher introduces a problem-

Population Explosion!

But what about the rate of Agriculture production?

Students make their personal opinion generally, Teacher divides them into their basic groups, Provides reading materials on the same subject

After group level discussion, presentation and reach at Conclusion.

SEMINAR

A class level seminar is to be conducted on

What will happen if this low rate of production continue like this?

Teacher awaken the students in this regard by showing a **Chart on the population growth** and **food production**.

Followed by general discussion on the same.

Teacher divides them into 5 groups and they discuss the various problems to be faced by the state of Kerala in this regard and possible solutions.

Findings of each group are presented through a class level seminar.

Hai Posters!

All groups have to prepare posters on the scheduled seminar and have to exhibit it

Report

All students have to prepare a Seminar report on it.

Have to raise slogans

Teacher and students together say a slogan related to the need for having a cordial way of living. Students prepare themselves individual slogans on the same subject.

Bullettin board

They have to exhibit their slogans on it. Have a self evaluation to find the best slogans.Teacher congratulates the winner.

Standard IX

NUTRITION IN PLANTS

Curriculum Objectives

☞ Through observation and reference the students were aware themselves the importance of plants as the providers of food for other living things. Students have to develop a positive and friendly attitude towards protection of plants and environment and to make it as their life style.

➤ **Human Rights**

- Right to Environment
- Right to profession and improvement of environment and safeguarding of forest and wildlife.

Learning materials:

Learning Activities

I will say a story

Teacher says a story........

Once upon a time, there was a forest, it is full of trees. There was a very aged old tree. One day a wood cutter came to the forest. By seeing him all the trees were started to worry. The old tree asked them the reason, they said it was due to the arrival of the wood cutters. Old tree asked why they are so much afraid of him? Does he carry anything with him? "No", others said. So you don't affraid of him, old tree consoled everyone......

Teacher completes the story and asks the students to write a message that they wish to convey their fellowbeings regarding the need for the protection of plants. (Individual work). Some of them have to present it in the class, the best one with necessary modification has to be pasted on the school notice board.

Teacher brings a News paper—Report

"Dumping the waste and destroying the land"

One of the students, reads the news and discuss the destruction brought by various human activities towards the nature.

Analyse the News paper report.

Teacher divides the students in to groups and provides them news papers of different days. They have to nalyse the news and to find various news related to the human interruption in the nature's equlibrium.

Seminar Presentation

The groups will prepare a report on the destruction of the nature by the human activities and make group level discussion, can make necessary corrections in the seminar paper.

All groups have to give the necessary publicity for the seminar through posters, notices, preparing pamphlets etc.

Seminar presentation, discussion and conclusion. Each student has to write an individual seminar project, teacher evaluates and grades it.

Collage as Assignment

It is an individual activity, each has to prepare a collage on the following topic.

"Man and Existence of Nature"

They can prepare news collage, by collecting related articles from the news dailies, magazines etc. They paste it in their science diary. Exhibit in the class individually, all students pass them from one end to the other and observe and evaluate each one.

Celebrate World Environmental Day

June 5th the World Environmental Day

Teacher introduces it in the class, and discuss various activities to be done in the school. Plan and execute it.

Have a Procession

As a continuation of the above activities teacher and students plan for a procession, prepare placards, posters, slogans etc., The procession can be held with the collaboration of others also. Parent Teacher Association members can participate in it.

Make '10 commandments' to protect the Diversity of Living Things

An individual work, all write it, present it in the classroom. They select best 10 out of it and exhibit in the bulletin board of science club.

Have an environment friendly school

Teacher makes discussion with students to put it in to practice those 10 commandments in the school, prepare a design and execute it.

Standard X

EVOLUTION

Curriculum Objectives

☞ Students have to know about the chromosomal abberation, mutations that lead to human and animal body disorders.

➤ **Human Rights**

- Right to Environment
- Right to Life
- Right of the Child

Learning materials:

Learning Activities

Observe and find out

Teacher shows a chart with pictures on it (normal man and man with chromosomal disorders). Students observe and compare the differences in the pictures.

Students present their observations in the classroom

Teacher introduces the subject mutation.

Mutations, how it causes?

Teacher presents a rolling chart with certain causes written on it for mutation. Students observe it and write their personal opinion on it.

Have a group discussion

Teacher divides the students in to groups and give a few discussion questions on mutation and its effects. Students have to answer the questions through wider discussions and references.

Discussions will be completed and each group will present their observation that lead to class level discussion and teacher concludes it.

PHYSICS

Standard VIII **Unit: Wave motion**

REASON FOR TSUNAMI

Curriculum Objectives

- ☞ To know about Tsunami and seasmic waves.
- ☞ To know about the seasmic waves and Tsunami waves through experiences and pictures.

➤ **Human Rights**

- Right to life
- Right to environment
- Right to education

Activities : The Giant Sea

Children are given the reports in news papers and photos of tsunami of 26th December 2004. They are asked to note the cause of tsunami and the reason for not reducing the death rate.

II. What are the reasons?

Facts	Reasons
1. The waves rised upto 20m	....
2. The sea come to the land about kilometers	....

III. Photo exhibition

Students collect maximum photos about Tsunami.
They exhibit on bullettin board.

IV. Seminars

Seminar is conducting about wave motion and seasmic waves by professionals. Students are grouped and discussed about it.

V. Is it denying rights? Discussion

A discussion is conducting on the accidents caused by the accidebtal arrival of tsunami waves and irresponsibility of the authorities.

VI. Poster making

Awareness programmes are conducting for fishermen about the natural calamities like tsunami. Poster making, small discussions, photo exhibition, speech etc are organising.

Standard IX **Unit: Light**

INFRA RED AND ULTRAVIOLET RADIATION

Curriculum Objectives

- ☞ To know about Infra Red and Ultra Violet radiation
- ☞ To know about the harmful effects of Infra Red and Ultra violet radiations.

➤ **Human Rights**

- Right to human life
- Right to enjoy the highest standards of physical and mental health.

Activity I

Students are divided into 7 groups and are named according to the colours in the spectrum of sunlight. They are asked to discuss the invisible rays coming from Sun.

They also discuss the use of Infra red and Ultra violet rays.

Activity II

Students collect the information from paper cuttings and CDs and finds out the harmful effects of Ultraviolet rays.

Activity III

Students discuss the solution to decrease the quality of Ultra violet rays in the earth. They find out the human rights which are denied, with the help of the charts.

Standard X **Unit: Production and distribution of Electricity**

DIFFERENT TYPES OF POWER STATIONS

Curriculum Objectives

☞ To know about different types of power stations and their working.

☞ To know about the changes of nature due to construction of power stations.

➤ **Human Rights**

- Right to environment
- Right to social security
- Right to enjoy the highest standards of physical and mental health.
- Right to life

Activity I

Divides students into three groups and asks them to discuss the functioning of power stations. Also ask them to discuss the harmful effects to nature due to their constructions.

Activity II

Students are asked to list out the difficulties caused by the construction of power stations in animals.

Activity III

From these the students find out the human rights which has been violoated. They make a chart of it and present.

CHEMISTRY

Standard VIII **Unit: Water**

DETERGENTS

Curriculum Objectives

- To know the hardness of water.
- To discriminate the action of soap and detergent in hard water.
- To know the environmental problems caused by detergents and to conduct awareness programmes against it.

➤ **Human Rights**

- Right to environment
- Right to social security
- Right to right selection

Activities

I. Can you answer?

Teacher presents a riddle in the class room
............Still in the form of nice powder
I'm fine to remove the dirt
I'll dissolve in all water
But the environment hates me............
— *Can you say who am I?*
Children answer the question—detergent

Activity II

Much more questions

Teacher give the 'reference card' regarding the soaps and detergents to the children in the group. They make as many questions as possible from that reference card. Teacher value the questions.

Activity III

Question War:

The children conduct a Question War- mutually regarding the question they made. The teacher give certain relevant answers to the questions, if necessary.

IV. Field Trip

a) Visit a detergent company. Also visit ten houses situated near the factory. Try to understand the difficulties they suffer- by a friendly talk and note down.
b) Study the problems of the people who use the detergent in their home with the help of a survey (questionnaire given) and make a report.

V. Debate

Is the detergent an enemy or friend?

Conducting an open debate. A child is selected for controlling the debate. Arguments should come strongly. Debate ends by giving an awareness about the pollution caused by the detergents.

Standard IX **Unit: Chemistry in everyday life**

SOFT DRINKS AND CHEMISTRY

Curriculum Objectives

- To identify different types of soft drinks we get from shops and to know its components.
- To make aware about the harmful effect of soft drinks
- To make aware about the human rights which we are not enjoying by using softdrinks.

➤ **Human Rights**

- Right to Health
- Right to enjoyment

Learning Aids

1. Samples of soft driks
2. Paper cuttings
3. Questionnaire
4. Posters
5. Laboratory equipment

Activity I

Children are given paper cuttings containing production and harmful effects of soft drinks (Display on the bullettin board and say to read it)

Activity II

They are grouped and are given the names of different soft drinks. Each group finds out the ingredients of the drinks by examining the labels. They present it.

Activity III

Discuss about how the chemicals present in the soft drinks affect the body. Interviews are organising to make aware how extent these chemicals are useful to our body. Questionnaires are prepared for interview.

Activity IV

Taking samples of soft drinks and putting teeth, bones etc., in it and observing it. Recording results.

Activity V

Data are collecting through interviews. Making a report on the basis of these informations.

Activity VI

Presentation of report. Main points of the report presents and exhibits on the chart.

Activity VII

Physical, economical and environmental problems caused by soft drinks are obtained from different sources.

Activity VIII

Posters are prepared for making aware the harmful effects of soft drinks. They are exhibiting after discussion.

Standard X **Unit: Chemistry in Everyday life**

CEMENT

Curriculum Objectives

- To know about the production of cement
- To make aware about the environmental problems caused by the raw materials used for manufacturing cement.
- To know the problems caused by cement factories.

➤ **Human Rights**

- Right to Life
- Right to environment
- Right to work
- Right to enjoy the highest standards of physical and mental health.

Learning Aids

Charts, CDs

A field trip to Malabar Cement Factory in Valayar in Palghat district.

Activity I

Students are asked to discuss and present the different steps and raw materials of the manufacture of cement as per the information got from the field trip.

Activity II

Students gets an idea about the environmental problems due to the collection of raw materials for cement production. Air pollution, problems of factory employees etc. are discussed and noted. Violoated human rights are discussed as per the data from news papers and CDs. A Seminar is organised based on this.

Annexure

Human Rights—New Trends

RIGHT TO ENVIRONMENT

This is the age of environmental consciousness. As reported by Mac Donald (1991) the environmental protection has become big business. A recent newsletter says "A new directory shows companies how to tap into the billions of dollars available from the US government, foreign governments and multilateral lending institutions to support environmentally sound trade and investment". There are also astonishing numbers of international instruments with environmental protection their aim.

But this does not mean that the environmental problems of the world are solved. Let us examine some of the recent events related to our Environment as reported by Mac Donald.

1. There is very wide acceptance that some degree of "global warming" is now inevitable; the consequent rise in sea-level may flood very considerable areas of Bangladesh, and low lying countries such as Maldives and Tuvalu could cease to exist. (1990 was the warmest year since records began).
2. It is estimated that in Uganda, in 1981 it was necessary to travel over four times as far to find firewood as it had been in 1966.
3. The Narmada dam scheme in India will displace more than one million people, destroy over 50,000 hectares of forest, probably wipe out some species of fauna and flora and encourage the spread of waterborne diseases.
4. About 2 in 3 Australians who live up to 70 suffer from skin cancer once in their lives and figures for malignant skin cancer are rising; the depletion of the ozone layer which has already occurred is expected to increase skin cancer among Australians by 12 to 20%.
5. In 1989, despite a general improvement, Hong Kong experienced its worst "red tide", caused by the impact of pollution on marine

life: the sale of shellfish in the affected area was banned for 2 weeks because of the risk of poisoning.

Environmental damage is peculiarly unlimited by boundaries of space or even time, Noise pollution perhaps has little extra-territorial impact, but water and air pollution, deforestation and desertification will often affect several countries. And over-use of resources, pollution, all the things involved in non-sustainable development, have implications for all future generations.

The issues which have attracted the most widespread interest and concern in recent years have included firstly the depletion of the ozone layer, and the actual hole over the Antarctic, caused by CFC and other chemicals, which, as well as increasing the incidence of skin cancer, may have climatic implications. Those chemicals are also "greenhouse gases" and have been playing their part with the gases produced by the burning of fossil fuels, and with methane in producing a state of affairs which many, if not all, scientists predict will lead to a raising of the earth's temperature and of the levels of the oceans.

The former could cause such changes in grain production in grain growing areas that famine may affect many Third World countries. The latter, as well as possibly obliterating some small low-lying states will cause serious flooding problems in Australia, Canada and the United Kingdom. Recent research in Canada suggests that warming may already be having an effect: in northern Ontario it was found that forest fires had increased, rain and snow reduced, and fish had taken to swimming at a greater depth to avoid the warm surface water of lakes.

Acid rain, much discussed in Europe and North America, has also been detected in India. Acid rain is caused by the emission of oxides of nitrogen and sulphur dioxide into the atmosphere from, for example, smelting. And causes damage to trees, to buildings and to river and lake waters and the fish they contain.

The destruction of the tropical rain forests has been the focus of much media attention. Most attention has been on the impact this has on the greenhouse effect (because this will affect the affluent countries of the world almost as much as the poor). But the permanent loss of many species of life, including those which might be of potential value to man, and the destruction of the way of life of forest residents are also matters of major concern.

Destruction of forests and vegetation generally has been going on for as long as man has had tools; it causes the loss of topsoil and therefore of fertility; the soil itself may be deposited elsewhere, such as the Bay of Bengal, where it causes flooding, or into reservoirs their capacity.

The courts of India, at least, have been able to erect on the foundation of a right to life protection against environmental degradation. "The slow poisoning by the polluted atmosphere caused by environmental pollution and spoliation should also be regarded as amounting to violation of Art. 21 of the Constitution" said one High Court in India and recently the Indian Supreme Court held that the right to life includes "the right to enjoyment of pollution-free water and air"

Environmental rights mesh with other sorts of rights in various ways.

They are often perceived as conflicting with developmental needs, and the emphasis on "development" has led in many countries, both "developed" and "developing", capitalist and socialist, to environmental considerations being neglected because they were assumed to conflict with development.

Some of the important articles and principles related to the right to Environment are listed below :

Universal Declaration of Human Rights

Article 3

Everyone has the right to life

Declaration of the United Nations Conference on the Human Environment,

Stockholm 16 June 1971

Principle 1

Man has the fundamental right to freedom, equality and adequate conditions of life, in an environment of quality that permits a life of dignity and well-being...

International Covenant on Economic. Social and Cultural Rights

Article 12

The States Parties to the present Covenant recognize the right of everyone to the enjoyment of the highest attainable standard of physical and mental health.

The steps to be taken by the States Parties...to achieve the full realization of this right shall include those necessary for ...(b). The improvement of all aspects of environmental and industrial hygiene.

UN General Assembly resolution on the World charter for nature,

28 October 1982

General Principle 1.

Nature shall be respected and its essential processes shall not be impaired

Constitution of India

Article 48 A

The state shall endeavour to protect and improve the environment and to safeguard the forests and wild life of the country

RIGHTS OF THE CHILD

The Convention on the Rights of Children was adopted in 1989, in recognition of the fact that in all countries, there are children living in exceptionally difficult conditions, who need special protection. The Convention seeks to assure to all children most of the rights and freedoms guaranteed in the International Bill of Rights, like life, liberty, the freedom of expression and conscience,non discrimination, and privacy.

Fundamental Principles

Respect for the Child's Opinion

The corollary to children as subjects of rights is the principle that their opinion should be respected. It means that the child has the right to freedom of expression, freedom of thought, freedom of conscience and freedom of assembly.

Each Child has Rights

The recognition that children have equal value as adults implies that each child has rights. The principle that all children should enjoy rights is fundamental to the Convention. The principle is based on the notion that children are subjects and not objects of the rights. Moreover, children should enjoy their rights without discrimination. It means that girls should be given the same opportunities as the boys. Similarly, disabled children and children of disadvantageous groups should enjoy the same rights as others.

Equal Value as Human Beings

An underlying principle of the Convention is that of according children the same value as adults. This principle stresses that childhood has value in itself. It is not merely a preparatory stage for adulthood. The implication of this principle is that the society has an obligation to create conditions for the child to enjoy his or her childhood.

Best Interests of the Child

While children have equal value as grownups they also need the protection and support from the society for enjoying their childhood. The principle of best interests of the child balances the need for providing protection to children while respecting.

This principle is most clearly stated in article 3 (1) of the Convention.

'In all actions concerning children, whether undertaken by public or private social welfare institutions, courts of law, administrative authorities or legislative bodies, the best interests of the child shall be a primary consideration'.

The interests of the child take precedent over the interests of parents or the state. The principle as stated in article 3 (1) applies to 'all actions concerning children' and not restricted to legal or administrative proceedings.

The following section provides the details of the articles of the convention.

PART 1

Article 1 : *Definition of a child

For the purposes of the present Convention, a child means every human being below the age of eighteen years unless, under the law applicable to the child, majority is attained earlier.

Article 2 : Non-discrimination

1. States Parties shall respect and ensure the rights set forth in the present Convention to each child within their jurisdiction without discrimination of any kind, irrespective of the child's or his or her parent's or legal guardian's race, colour, sex, language, religion, political or other opinion, national, ethnic or social origin, property, disability, birth or other status.
2. States Parties shall take all appropriate measures to ensure that the child is protected against all forms of discrimination or punishment on the basis of the status, activities, expressed opinions, or beliefs of the child's parents, legal guardians, or family members.

Article 3 : Best interests of the child

1. In all actions concerning children, whether undertaken by public or private social welfare institutions, courts of law. Administrative authorities or legislative bodies, the best interests of the child shall be a primary consideration.
2. States Parties undertake to ensure the child such protection and care as is necessary for his or her well-being, taking into account the rights and duties of his or her parents, legal guardians, or other individuals legally responsible for him or her, and to this end, shall take all appropriate legislative and administrative measures.
3. States Parties shall ensure that the institutions, services and facilities responsible for the care or protection of children shall conform with the standards established by competent authorities, particularly in the areas of safety, health, in the number and suitability of their staff as well as competent supervision.

Article 4 : Implementation of rights

States Parties shall undertake all appropriate legislative. Administrative, and other measure for the implementation of the rights recognized in the present Convention. With regard to economic, social and cultural rights, States Parties shall undertake such measures to the maximum extent of their available resources and, where needed, within the framework of international co-operation.

Article 5 : Parental guidance and the child's evolving capacities

States Parties shall respect the responsibilities, rights and duties of parents or, where applicable, the members of the extended family or community as provided for by local custom, legal guardians or other persons legally responsible for the child, to provide, in a manner consistent with the evolving capacities of the child, appropriate direction and guidance in the exercise by the child of the rights recognised in the present Convention.

Article 6 : Survival and development

1. States Parties recognize that every child has the inherent right to life.
2. States Parties shall ensure to the maximum extent possible the survival and development of the child.

Article 7 : Name and nationality

1. The child shall be registered immediately after birth and shall have the right from birth to name, the right to acquire a nationality and, as far as possible, the right to know and be cared for by his or her parents.

2. States Parties shall ensure the implementation of these rights in accordance with their national law and their obligations under the relevant international instruments in this field, in particular where the child would other-wise be stateless.

Article 8 : Preservation of identity

1. States Parties undertake to respect the right of the child to reserve his/ her identity, including nationality, name and family relations as recognized by law without unlawful interference.

2. Where a child is illegally deprived of some or all of the elements of his or her identity. States Parties shall provide appropriate assistance and protection as a view to speedily re-establishing his or her identity.

Article 9 : Separation from parents

This article provides that ordinarily a child shall not be separated from his or her parents. Articles 9 permits separation of a child from his or her parents if it is required for the best interests of the child. However, competent authorities under relevant laws should decide it and such decisions should be subject to judicial review. The child who is separated from one or both parents has a right to maintain personal relations and direct contact with both parents, except if it is contrary to the child's best interests.

Article 10 : Family reunification

This article stipulates that States should facilitate reunification of families by permitting travel into, or out of their territories. This right is subject to limitations when necessary to protect the national security, public order (ordre public), public health or morals or the rights and freedoms of others. The limitations imposed should be based on law and consistent with the rights recognized in the present Convention.

Article 11 : Illicit transfer and non-return

1. States Parties shall take measures to combat the illicit transfer stands non-return of children abroad.

2. To this end, States Parties shall promote the conclusion of bilateral or multilateral agreements or accession to existing agreements.

Article 12 : The child's opinion

1. States Parties shall assure to the child who is capable of forming his or her own views the right to express those views freely in all matters affecting the child, the views of the child being giving due weight in accordance with the age and maturity of the child.

2. For this purpose, the child shall in particular be provided the opportunity to be heard in any judicial and administrative proceedings affecting the child, either directly, or through a representative or an appropriate body, in a manner consistent with the procedural rules of national law.

Article 13 : Freedom of expression

1. The child shall have the right to freedom of expression; this right shall include freedom to seek, receive and impart information and ideas of all kinds, regardless of frontiers, either orally, in writing or in print, in the form of art, or through any other media of the child's choice.

2. The exercise of this right may be subject to certain restrictions, but these shall only be such as are provided by law and are necessary;

(a) For respect of the rights or reputations of others; or

(b) For the protection of national security or of public order (ordre public), or of public health or morals.

Article 14 : Freedom of thought, conscience and religion

This article guarantees the right of the child to freedom of thought, conscience and religion. The State should also respect the rights and duties of parents to provide direction to the child in a manner consistent with the evolving capacities of the child. This right is subject to limitations when necessary to protect public safety, order, health or morals or the fundamental rights and freedoms of others.

Article 15 : Freedom of association

1. States Parties recognize the rights of the child to freedom of association and to freedom of peaceful assembly.

2. No restrictions may be placed on the exercise of these rights other than those imposed in conformity with the law and which are necessary in a democratic society in the interests of national security or public safety, public order (ordre public), the protection of public health or morals or the protection of the rights and freedoms of others.

Article 16 : Protection of privacy

1. No child shall be subjected to arbitrary or unlawful interference with his or her privacy, family home or correspondence, nor to unlawful attacks on his or her honour and reputation.

2. The child has the right to the protection of the law against such interference or attacks.

Article 17 : Access to appropriate information

Article 17 recognizes the importance of mass media and requires that State parties ensure that the child has access to information and material from a diversity of sources. State parties are also required to encourage mass media to disseminate information and material of benefit to children. In addition, State parties should develop appropriate guidelines for protecting the child from material harmful to his well-being.

Article 18 : Parental responsibilities

This article acknowledges the principle that the primary responsibility for the upbringing and the development of the child rests with both parents or legal guardians. The best interests of the child will be their primary concern. The State should develop institutions, facilities and services for the care of children o assist parents or legal guardians to perform their child-rearing responsibilities. States parties should also take measures to ensure that children of working parents benefit from child-care services and facilities.

Article 19 : Protection from abuse and neglect

Article 19 obligates State parties to take legislative, administrative, social and educational measures to protect the child from physical or mental abuse, neglect, exploitation including sexual abuse by parents or others responsible for the care of the child. The State parties should also take measures to develop social programmes for prevention of abuse and treatment of victims.

Article 20 : Protection of children without families

This article requires that State Parties provide special protection and assistance to a child deprived of his or her family environment. State parties should provide alternative care for such a child including adoption or institutional placement. In providing such alternative, care, the State should take into account the child's ethnic, religious, cultural and linguistic background.

Article 21 : Adoption

This article stipulates that those States Parties that recognize or permit adoption should ensure that it is carried out in the best interests of the child. Competent authorities according to the relevant law should authorize all adoption. Article 21 recognizes inter country adoption. However, they should enjoy safeguards and standards similar to national adoption.

Article 22 : Refugee children

Article 22 provides that State Parties take measures to provide protection and humanitarian assistance to a refugee child or a child seeking refugee status.

Article 23 : Disabled children

The article requires that State Parties recognize that a mentally or physically disabled child should enjoy a full and decent life in dignity and promote their self-reliance and active participation in the community. Disabled children shall have the right to special treatment, education and care.

Article 24 : Health and health services

Article 24 stipulates that State Parties recognize the right of the child to the enjoyment of the highest attainable standard of health and to treatment of illness and rehabilitation of health, 'State parties shall strive to ensure that no child is deprived of his or her right of access to such health care services'.

In implementing this right, State Parties should take measures to diminish infant and child mortality, development of primary health care, to combat disease and malnutrition, ensure pre-natal and post-natal health care for mothers and abolish traditional practices that harm the health of the children.

Article 25 : Periodic review of placement

States Parties recognize the right of a child who has been placed by the competent authorities for the purposes of care, protection, or treatment of his or her physical or mental health, to a periodic review of the treatment provided to the child and all other circumstances relevant to his or her placement.

Article 26 : Social security

1. States Parties shall recognize for every child the right to benefit from social security, including social insurance, and shall take the necessary measures to achieve the full realization of this right in accordance with their national law.

2. The benefits should, where appropriate, be granted, taking into account the resources and the circumstances of the child and persons having responsibility for the maintenance of the child, as well as any other consideration relevant to an application for benefits made by or on behalf of the child.

Article 27 : Standard of living

This article recognizes the right of every child to a standard of living adequate for the child's physical, mental, spiritual, moral and social development. The parents have the primary responsibility to ensure the standard of living adequate for the child's development. The State parties should provide assistance including where necessary material assistance to enable parents to implement this right.

Article 28 : Education

Article 28 provides that State parties recognize the right of the child to education. To realize this right, they shall make primary education free and compulsory. They will also encourage different forms of secondary education and make them accessible to every child by providing it free or offering financial assistance. States parties shall take measures to ensure that school discipline is administered in conformity with a child's dignity and rights.

Article 29 : Aims of Education

This article requires that the education of the child shall be directed to the development of the child's personality, talents and mental and physical abilities. It should prepare the child for leading a responsible life in a free society. It should also foster respect for his or her parents, his or her own cultural identity, other cultures and for human rights and fundamental freedoms.

Article 30 : Children of minorities or indigenous peoples

In those States in which ethnic, religious or linguistic minorities or persons of indigenous origin exist, a child belonging to such a minority or who is indigenous shall not be denied the right, in community with other members of his or her group, to enjoy his or her own culture, to profess and practice his or her own religion, or to use his or her own language.

Article 31 : Leisure, recreation and cultural activities

1. States parties recognize the right of the child to rest and leisure, to engage in play and recreational activities appropriate to the age of the child and to participate freely in cultural life and the arts.

2. States Parties shall respect and promote the right of the child to participate fully in cultural an artistic life and shall encourage the provision of appropriate and equal opportunities for cultural, artistic, recreational and leisure activity.

Article 32 : Child labour

1. States Parties recognize the right of the child to be protected from economic exploitation and from performing any work that is likely to be hazardous or to interfere with the child's education, or to be harmful to the child's health or physical, mental, spiritual, moral or social development.

2. States Parties shall take legislative, administrative, social and educational measures to ensure the implementa-tion of the present article. To this end, and having regard to the relevant provisions of the international instruments.

States Parties shall in particular:

(a) Provide for a minimum age or minimum ages for admission to employment;
(b) Provide for appropriate regulation of the hours and conditions of employment;
(c) Provide for appropriate penalties or other sanctions to ensure the effective enforcement of the present article.

Article 33 : Drug abuse

States Parties shall take all appropriate measures, including legislative, administrative, social and educational measures, to protect children from the illicit use of narcotic drugs and psychotropic substances as defined in the relevant international treaties, and to prevent the use of children in the illicit production and trafficking of such substances.

Article 34 : Sexual exploitation

States Parties undertake to protect the child from all forms of sexual exploitation and sexual abuse. For these purposes, States Parties shall in particular take all appropriate national, bilateral and multilateral measures to prevent:

(a) The inducement or coercion of a child to engage in any unlawful sexual activity;
(b) The exploitative use of children in prostitution or other unlawful sexual practices;
(c) The exploitative use of children in pornographic performances and materials.

Article 35 : Sale, trafficking and abduction

States Parties shall take all appropriate national, bilateral and multilateral measures to prevent the abduction of, the sale of or traffic in children for any purpose or in any form.

Article 36 : Other forms of exploitation

States Parties shall protect the child against all other forms of exploitation prejudicial to any aspects of the child's welfare.

Article 37 : Torture and deprivation of liberty

This article provides that no child shall be subjected to torture or other cruel, inhuman or degrading treatment or punishment. No capital punishment or life imprisonment with-out the possibility of release shall be imposed on persons below 18 years.

This article also prohibits unlawful or arbitrary deprivation of the liberty of any child. The Convention does not ban the imprisonment of minors. But the arrest, detention and imprisonment of young offenders should bc used as a last measure and for the shortest possible time. Every child deprived of his or her liberty should be treated with humanity and in particular separated from adults unless it is done in the child's best interest. Every child deprived of his or her liberty shall have legal and other assistance and the reason to challenge the legality of the deprivation of his or her liberty before a court or other authority.

Article 38 : Armed conflict

1. States Parties undertake to respect and to ensure respect for rules of international humanitarian law applicable to them in armed conflicts which are relevant to the child.

2. States Parties shall take all feasible measures to ensure that persons who have not attained the age of fifteen years do not take a direct part in hostilities.
3. States Parties shall refrain from recruiting any person who has not attained the age of fifteen years into their armed forces. In recruiting among those persons who have attained the age of fifteen years but who have not attained the age of eighteen years, States Parties shall endeavour to give priority to those who are oldest.
4. In accordance with their obligations under international humanitarian law to protect the civilian population in armed conflicts, States Parties shall take all feasible measures to ensure protection and care of children who are affected by an armed conflict.

Article 39 : Rehabilitative care

States Parties shall take all appropriate measures to promote physical and psychological recovery and social reintegration of a child victim of any form of neglect exploitation or abuse. Torture or any other form of cruel, inhuman or degrading treatment or punishment; or armed conflicts. Such recovery and reintegration shall take place in an environment which fosters the health, self-respect and dignity of the child.

Article 40 : Administration of juvenile justice

This article provides for safeguards in the administration of juvenile justice. Every child alleged as, or accused of infringing the penal law has the right to treatment consistent with the promotion of the child's sense of dignity and worth.

In the administration of juvenile justice, State parties shall ensure the respect for the principle that no one shall be held guiltily of any criminal offence on account of any act or omission which did not constitute a criminal offence, under national or international law, at that time when it was committed. State parties should also ensure the following guarantees:

1. Presumption of innocence;
2. Inform promptly and directly of the charges against him or her;
3. To determine the matter by a competent, independent and impartial authority or judicial body;
4. Not to compel to give testimony or confess guilt;
5. The right to review and appeal to a higher authority or judicial body;
6. To have free access to an interpreter if the child cannot understand or speak the language; and

7. To respect his or her privacy at all stages of the proceedings.

Article 41 : Respect for existing standards

Nothing in the present Convention shall affect any provisions which are more conducive to the realization of the rights of the child and which may be contained in;

(a) The law of a State Party; or

(a) International law in force for that State.

PART II

Implementation and entry into force

Article 42

It obligates State parties to make the principles and provisions of the Convention widely known by both adults and children alike.

The Convention on the Rights of the Child has 54 articles in all, but most of the rest are about how adults and governments should work together to make sure all children get all their rights.

Committee on the Rights of the Child (CRC)

The Convention sets up the Committee on the Rights of the Child consisting of ten independent members to monitor the State Parties compliance of their obligations under the Covenant. The Convention is the only treaty that accords a role of Non Governmental Organisations assisting the Committee to monitor the compliance of State Parties' obligations.

CONVENTION CONCERNING THE PROHIBITION AND IMMEDIATE ACTION FOR THE ELIMINATION OF THE WORST FORMS OF CHILD LABOUR

(Adopted by the Conference at its Eighty-seventh session, Geneva, 17 June 1999)

Convention 182:

The General Conference of the International Labour Organization,

Having been convened at Geneva by the Governing Body of the InternationalLabourOffice, and having met in its 87th Session on 1 June 1999, and

Considering the need to adopt new instruments for the prohibition and elimination of the worst forms of child labour, as the main priority for national and international action, including international cooperation and assistance, to complement the Convention and the Recommendation concerning Minimum Age for Admission to Employment, 1973, which remain fundamental instruments on child labour, and

Considering that the effective elimination of the worst forms of child labour requires immediate and comprehensive action, taking into account the importance of free basic education and the need to remove the children concerned from all such work and to provide for their rehabilitation and social integration while addressing the needs of their families, and

Recalling the resolution concerning the elimination of child labour adopted by the International Labour Conference at its 83rd Session in 1996, and

Recognizing that child labour is to a great extent caused by poverty and that the long-term solution lies in sustained economic growth leading to social progress, in particular poverty alleviation and universal education, and

Recalling the Convention on the Rights of the Child adopted by the United Nations General Assembly on 20 November 1989, and

Recalling the ILO Declaration on Fundamental Principles and Rights at Work and its Follow-up, adopted by the International Labour Conference at its 86th Session in 1998, and

Recalling that some of the worst forms of child labour are covered by other international instruments, in particular the Forced Labour Convention, 1930, and the United Nations Supplementary Convention on the Abolition of Slavery, the Slave Trade, and Institutions and Practices Similar to Slavery, 1956, and

*Having decide*d upon the adoption of certain proposals with regard to child labour, which is the fourth item on the agenda of the session, and

Having determined that these proposals shall take the form of an international Convention;

Adopts this seventeenth day of June of the year one thousand nine hundred and ninety-nine the following Convention, which may be cited as the Worst Forms of Child Labour Convention, 1999.

Article 1

Each Member which ratifies this Convention shall take immediate and effective measures to secure the prohibition and elimination of the worst forms of child labour as a matter of urgency.

Article 2

For the purposes of this Convention, the term "child" shall apply to all persons under the age of 18.

Article 3

For the purposes of this Convention, the term "the worst forms of child labour" comprises:

all forms of slavery or practices similar to slavery, such as the sale and trafficking of children, debt bondage and serfdom and forced or compulsory labour, including forced or compulsory recruitment of children for use in armed conflict;

the use, procuring or offering of a child for prostitution, for the production of pornography or for pornographic performances;

the use, procuring or offering of a child for illicit activities, in particular for the production and trafficking of drugs as defined in the relevant international treaties;

work which, by its nature or the circumstances in which it is carried out, is likely to harm thc health, safety or morals of children.

Article 4

The types of work referred to under Article 3(d) shall be determined by national laws or regulations or by the competent authority, after consultation with the organizations of employers and workers concerned, taking into consideration relevant international standards, in particular Paragraphs 3 and 4 of the Worst Forms of Child Labour Recommendation, 1999.

The competent authority, after consultation with the organizations of employers and workers concerned, shall identify where the types of work so determined exist.

The list of the types of work determined under paragraph 1 of this Article shall be periodically examined and revised as necessary, in consultation with the organizations of employers and workers concerned.

Article 5

Each Member shall, after consultation with employers' and workers' organizations, establish or designate appropriate mechanisms to monitor the implementation of the provisions giving effect to this Convention.

Article 6

Each Member shall design and implement programmes of action to eliminate as a priority the worst forms of child labour.

Such programmes of action shall be designed and implemented in consultation with relevant government institutions and employers' and workers' organizations, taking into consideration the views of other concerned groups as appropriate.

Article 7

Each Member shall take all necessary measures to ensure the effective implementation and enforcement of the provisions giving effect to this Convention including the provision and application of penal sanctions or, as appropriate, other sanctions.

Each Member shall, taking into account the importance of education in eliminating child labour, take effective and time-bound measures to:

prevent the engagement of children in the worst forms of child labour;

provide the necessary and appropriate direct assistance for the removal of children from the worst forms of child labour and for their rehabilitation and social integration;

ensure access to free basic education, and, wherever possible and appropriate, vocational training, for all children removed from the worst forms of child labour;

identify and reach out to children at special risk; and

take account of the special situation of girls.

Each Member shall designate the competent authority responsible for the implementation of the provisions giving effect to this Convention.

Article 8

Members shall take appropriate steps to assist one another in giving effect to the provisions of this Convention through enhanced international cooperation and/or assistance including support for social and economic development, poverty eradication programmes and universal education.

Article 9

The formal ratifications of this Convention shall be communicated to the Director-General of the International Labour Office for registration.

Article 10

This Convention shall be binding only upon those Members of the International Labour Organization whose ratifications have been registered with the Director-General of the International Labour Office.

It shall come into force 12 months after the date on which the ratifications of two Members have been registered with the Director-General.

Thereafter, this Convention shall come into force for any Member 12 months after the date on which its ratification has been registered.

Article 11

A Member which has ratified this Convention may denounce it after the expiration of ten years from the date on which the Convention first comes into force, by an act communicated to the Director-General of the International Labour Office for registration. Such denunciation shall not take effect until one year after the date on which it is registered.

Each Member which has ratified this Convention and which does not, within the year following the expiration of the period of ten years mentioned in the preceding paragraph, exercise the right of denunciation provided for in this Article, will be bound for another period of ten years and, thereafter, may denounce this Convention at the expiration of each period of ten years under the terms provided for in this Article.

Article 12

The Director-General of the International Labour Office shall notify all Members of the International Labour Organization of the registration of all ratifications and acts of denunciation communicated by the Members of the Organization.

When notifying the Members of the Organization of the registration of the second ratification, the Director-General shall draw the attention of the Members of the Organization to the date upon which the Convention shall come into force.

Article 13

The Director-General of the International Labour Office shall communicate to the Secretary-General of the United Nations, for registration in accordance with article 102 of the Charter of the United Nations, full particulars of all ratifications and acts of denunciation registered by the Director-General in accordance with the provisions of the preceding Articles.

Article 14

At such times as it may consider necessary, the Governing Body of the International Labour Office shall present to the General Conference a report on the working of this Convention and shall examine the desirability of placing on the agenda of the Conference the question of its revision in whole or in part.

Article 15

Should the Conference adopt a new Convention revising this Convention in whole or in part, then, unless the new Convention otherwise provides—

the ratification by a Member of the new revising Convention shall ipso jure involve the immediate denunciation of this Convention, notwithstanding the provisions of Article 11 above, if and when the new revising Convention shall have come into force;

as from the date when the new revising Convention comes into force, this Convention shall cease to be open to ratification by the Members.

This Convention shall in any case remain in force in its actual form and content for those Members which have ratified it but have not ratified the revising Convention.

Article 16

The English and French versions of the text of this Convention are equally authoritative.

OPTIONAL PROTOCOL TO THE CONVENTION ON THE RIGHTS OF THE CHILD ON THE SALE OF CHILDREN, CHILD PROSTITUTION AND CHILD PORNOGRAPHY

(Adopted and opened for signature, ratification and accession by General Assembly resolution A/RES/54/263 of 25 May 2000 entered into force on 18 January 2002)

The States Parties to the present Protocol,

Considering that, in order further to achieve the purposes of the Convention on the Rights of the Child and the implementation of its provisions, especially articles 1, 11, 21, 32, 33, 34, 35 and 36, it would be appropriate to extend the measures that States Parties should undertake in order to guarantee the protection of the child from the sale of children, child prostitution and child pornography,

Considering also that the Convention on the Rights of the Child recognizes the right of the child to be protected from economic exploitation and from performing any work that is likely to be hazardous or to interfere with the child's education, or to be harmful to the child's health or physical, mental, spiritual, moral or social development,

Gravely concerned at the significant and increasing international traffic in children for the purpose of the sale of children, child prostitution and child pornography,

Deeply concerned at the widespread and continuing practice of sex tourism, to which children are especially vulnerable, as it directly promotes the sale of children, child prostitution and child pornography,

Recognizing that a number of particularly vulnerable groups, including girl children, are at greater risk of sexual exploitation and that girl children are disproportionately represented among the sexually exploited,

Concerned about the growing availability of child pornography on the Internet and other evolving technologies, and recalling the International Conference on Combating Child Pornography on the Internet, held in Vienna in 1999, in particular its conclusion calling for the worldwide criminalization of the production, distribution, exportation, transmission, importation, intentional possession and advertising of child pornography, and stressing the importance of closer cooperation and partnership between Governments and the Internet industry,

Believing that the elimination of the sale of children, child prostitution and child pornography will be facilitated by adopting a holistic approach, addressing the contributing factors, including underdevelopment, poverty, economic disparities, inequitable socio-economic structure, dysfunctioning families, lack of education, urban-rural migration, gender discrimination, irresponsible adult sexual behaviour, harmful traditional practices, armed conflicts and trafficking in children,

Believing also that efforts to raise public awareness are needed to reduce consumer demand for the sale of children, child prostitution and child pornography, and believing further in the importance of strengthening global partnership among all actors and of improving law enforcement at the national level,

Noting the provisions of international legal instruments relevant to the protection of children, including the Hague Convention on Protection of Children and Cooperation in Respect of Intercountry Adoption, the Hague Convention on the Civil Aspects of International Child Abduction, the

Hague Convention on Jurisdiction, Applicable Law, Recognition, Enforcement and Cooperation in Respect of Parental Responsibility and Measures for the Protection of Children, and International Labour Organization Convention No. 182 on the Prohibition and Immediate Action for the Elimination of the Worst Forms of Child Labour,

Encouraged by the overwhelming support for the Convention on the Rights of the Child, demonstrating the widespread commitment that exists for the promotion and protection of the rights of the child,

Recognizing the importance of the implementation of the provisions of the Programme of Action for the Prevention of the Sale of Children, Child Prostitution and Child Pornography and the Declaration and Agenda for Action adopted at the World Congress against Commercial Sexual Exploitation of Children, held in Stockholm from 27 to 31 August 1996, and the other relevant decisions and recommendations of pertinent international bodies,

Taking due account of the importance of the traditions and cultural values of each people for the protection and harmonious development of the child, Have agreed as follows:

Article 1

States Parties shall prohibit the sale of children, child prostitution and child pornography as provided for by the present Protocol.

Article 2

For the purposes of the present Protocol:

(a) Sale of children means any act or transaction whereby a child is transferred by any person or group of persons to another for remuneration or any other consideration;

(b) Child prostitution means the use of a child in sexual activities for remuneration or any other form of consideration;

(c) Child pornography means any representation, by whatever means, of a child engaged in real or simulated explicit sexual activities or any representation of the sexual parts of a child for primarily sexual purposes.

Article 3

1. Each State Party shall ensure that, as a minimum, the following acts and activities are fully covered under its criminal or penal law, whether such offences are committed domestically or transnationally or on an individual or organized basis:

(a) In the context of sale of children as defined in article 2:

(i) Offering, delivering or accepting, by whatever means, a child for the purpose of:

a. Sexual exploitation of the child;

b. Transfer of organs of the child for profit;

c. Engagement of the child in forced labour;

(ii) Improperly inducing consent, as an intermediary, for the adoption of a child in violation of applicable international legal instruments on adoption;

(b) Offering, obtaining, procuring or providing a child for child prostitution, as defined in article 2;

(c) Producing, distributing, disseminating, importing, exporting, offering, selling or possessing for the above purposes child pornography as defined in article 2.

2. Subject to the provisions of the national law of a State Party, the same shall apply to an attempt to commit any of the said acts and to complicity or participation in any of the said acts.

3. Each State Party shall make such offences punishable by appropriate penalties that take into account their grave nature.

4. Subject to the provisions of its national law, each State Party shall take measures, where appropriate, to establish the liability of legal persons for offences established in paragraph 1 of the present article. Subject to the legal principles of the State Party, such liability of legal persons may be criminal, civil or administrative.

5. States Parties shall take all appropriate legal and administrative measures to ensure that all persons involved in the adoption of a child act in conformity with applicable international legal instruments.

Article 4

1. Each State Party shall take such measures as may be necessary to establish its jurisdiction over the offences referred to in article 3, paragraph 1, when the offences are commited in its territory or on board a ship or aircraft registered in that State.

2. Each State Party may take such measures as may be necessary to establish its jurisdiction over the offences referred to in article 3, paragraph 1, in the following cases:

(a) When the alleged offender is a national of that State or a person who has his habitual residence in its territory;

(b) When the victim is a national of that State.

3. Each State Party shall also take such measures as may be necessary to establish its jurisdiction over the aforementioned offences when the alleged offender is present in its territory and it does not extradite him or her to another State Party on the ground that the offence has been committed by one of its nationals.

4. The present Protocol does not exclude any criminal jurisdiction exercised in accordance with internal law.

Article 5

1. The offences referred to in article 3, paragraph 1, shall be deemed to be included as extraditable offences in any extradition treaty existing between States Parties and shall be included as extraditable offences in every extradition treaty subsequently concluded between them, in accordance with the conditions set forth in such treaties.

2. If a State Party that makes extradition conditional on the existence of a treaty receives a request for extradition from another State Party with which it has no extradition treaty, it may consider the present Protocol to be a legal basis for extradition in respect of such offences. Extradition shall be subject to the conditions provided by the law of the requested State.

3. States Parties that do not make extradition conditional on the existence of a treaty shall recognize such offences as extraditable offences between themselves subject to the conditions provided by the law of the requested State.

4. Such offences shall be treated, for the purpose of extradition between States Parties, as if they had been committed not only in the place in which they occurred but also in the territories of the States required to establish their jurisdiction in accordance with article 4.

5. If an extradition request is made with respect to an offence described in article 3, paragraph 1, and the requested State Party does not or will not extradite on the basis of the nationality of the offender, that State shall take suitable measures to submit the case to its competent authorities for the purpose of prosecution.

Article 6

1. States Parties shall afford one another the greatest measure of assistance in connection with investigations or criminal or extradition proceedings brought in respect of the offences set forth in article 3, paragraph 1, including assistance in obtaining evidence at their disposal necessary for the proceedings.

2. States Parties shall carry out their obligations under paragraph 1 of the present article in conformity with any treaties or other arrangements on mutual legal assistance that may exist between them. In the absence of such treaties or arrangements, States Parties shall afford one another assistance in accordance with their domestic law.

Article 7

States Parties shall, subject to the provisions of their national law:

(a) Take measures to provide for the seizure and confiscation, as appropriate, of:

(i) Goods, such as materials, assets and other instrumentalities used to commit or facilitate offences under the present protocol;

(ii) Proceeds derived from such offences;

(b) Execute requests from another State Party for seizure or confiscation of goods or proceeds referred to in subparagraph (a);

(c) Take measures aimed at closing, on a temporary or definitive basis, premises used to commit such offences.

Article 8

1. States Parties shall adopt appropriate measures to protect the rights and interests of child victims of the practices prohibited under the present Protocol at all stages of the criminal justice process, in particular by:

(a) Recognizing the vulnerability of child victims and adapting procedures to recognize their special needs, including their special needs as witnesses;

(b) Informing child victims of their rights, their role and the scope, timing and progress of the proceedings and of the disposition of their cases;

(c) Allowing the views, needs and concerns of child victims to be presented and considered in proceedings where their personal interests are affected, in a manner consistent with the procedural rules of national law;

(d) Providing appropriate support services to child victims throughout the legal process;

(e) Protecting, as appropriate, the privacy and identity of child victims and taking measures in accordance with national law to avoid the inappropriate dissemination of information that could lead to the identification of child victims;

(f) Providing, in appropriate cases, for the safety of child victims, as well as that of their families and witnesses on their behalf, from intimidation and retaliation;

(g) Avoiding unnecessary delay in the disposition of cases and the execution of orders or decrees granting compensation to child victims.

2. States Parties shall ensure that uncertainty as to the actual age of the victim shall not prevent the initiation of criminal investigations, including investigations aimed at establishing the age of the victim.

3. States Parties shall ensure that, in the treatment by the criminal justice system of children who are victims of the offences described in the present Protocol, the best interest of the child shall be a primary consideration.

4. States Parties shall take measures to ensure appropriate training, in particular legal and psychological training, for the persons who work with victims of the offences prohibited under the present Protocol.

5. States Parties shall, in appropriate cases, adopt measures in order to protect the safety and integrity of those persons and/or organizations involved in the prevention and/or protection and rehabilitation of victims of such offences.

6. Nothing in the present article shall be construed to be prejudicial to or inconsistent with the rights of the accused to a fair and impartial trial.

Article 9

1. States Parties shall adopt or strengthen, implement and disseminate laws, administrative measures, social policies and programmes to prevent the offences referred to in the present Protocol. Particular attention shall be given to protect children who are especially vulnerable to such practices.

2. States Parties shall promote awareness in the public at large, including children, through information by all appropriate means, education and training, about the preventive measures and harmful effects of the offences referred to in the present Protocol. In fulfilling their obligations under this article, States Parties shall encourage the participation of the community

and, in particular, children and child victims, in such information and education and training programmes, including at the international level.

3. States Parties shall take all feasible measures with the aim of ensuring all appropriate assistance to victims of such offences, including their full social reintegration and their full physical and psychological recovery.

4. States Parties shall ensure that all child victims of the offences described in the present Protocol have access to adequate procedures to seek, without discrimination, compensation for damages from those legally responsible.

5. States Parties shall take appropriate measures aimed at effectively prohibiting the production and dissemination of material advertising the offences described in the present Protocol.

Article 10

1. States Parties shall take all necessary steps to strengthen international cooperation by multilateral, regional and bilateral arrangements for the prevention, detection, investigation, prosecution and punishment of those responsible for acts involving the sale of children, child prostitution, child pornography and child sex tourism. States Parties shall also promote international cooperation and coordination between their authorities, national and international non-governmental organizations and international organizations.

2. States Parties shall promote international cooperation to assist child victims in their physical and psychological recovery, social reintegration and repatriation.

3. States Parties shall promote the strengthening of international cooperation in order to address the root causes, such as poverty and underdevelopment, contributing to the vulnerability of children to the sale of children, child prostitution, child pornography and child sex tourism.

4. States Parties in a position to do so shall provide financial, technical or other assistance through existing multilateral, regional, bilateral or other programmes.

Article 11

Nothing in the present Protocol shall affect any provisions that are more conducive to the realization of the rights of the child and that may be contained in:

(a) The law of a State Party;
(b) International law in force for that State.

Article 12

1. Each State Party shall, within two years following the entry into force of the present Protocol for that State Party, submit a report to the Committee on the Rights of the Child providing comprehensive information on the measures it has taken to implement the provisions of the Protocol.

2. Following the submission of the comprehensive report, each State Party shall include in the reports they submit to the Committee on the Rights of the Child, in accordance with article 44 of the Convention, any further information with respect to the implementation of the present Protocol. Other States Parties to the Protocol shall submit a report every five years.

3. The Committee on the Rights of the Child may request from States Parties further information relevant to the implementation of the present Protocol.

Article 13

1. The present Protocol is open for signature by any State that is a party to the Convention or has signed it.

2. The present Protocol is subject to ratification and is open to accession by any State that is a party to the Convention or has signed it. Instruments of ratification or accession shall be deposited with the Secretary- General of the United Nations.

Article 14

1. The present Protocol shall enter into force three months after the deposit of the tenth instrument of ratification or accession.

2. For each State ratifying the present Protocol or acceding to it after its entry into force, the Protocol shall enter into force one month after the date of the deposit of its own instrument of ratification or accession.

Article 15

1. Any State Party may denounce the present Protocol at any time by written notification to the Secretary- General of the United Nations, who shall thereafter inform the other States Parties to the Convention and all States that have signed the Convention. The denunciation shall take

effect one year after the date of receipt of the notification by the Secretary-General.

2. Such a denunciation shall not have the effect of releasing the State Party from its obligations under the present Protocol in regard to any offence that occurs prior to the date on which the denunciation becomes effective. Nor shall such a denunciation prejudice in any way the continued consideration of any matter that is already under consideration by the Committee on the Rights of the Child prior to the date on which the denunciation becomes effective.

Article 16

1. Any State Party may propose an amendment and file it with the Secretary-General of the United Nations. The Secretary-General shall thereupon communicate the proposed amendment to States Parties with a request that they indicate whether they favour a conference of States Parties for the purpose of considering and voting upon the proposals. In the event that, within four months from the date of such communication, at least one third of the States Parties favour such a conference, the Secretary-General shall convene the conference under the auspices of the United Nations. Any amendment adopted by a majority of States Parties present and voting at the conference shall be submitted to the General Assembly of the United Nations for approval.

2. An amendment adopted in accordance with paragraph 1 of the present article shall enter into force when it has been approved by the General Assembly and accepted by a two-thirds majority of States Parties.

3 When an amendment enters into force, it shall be binding on those States Parties that have accepted it, other States Parties still being bound by the provisions of the present Protocol and any earlier amendments they have accepted.

Article 17

1. The present Protocol, of which the Arabic, Chinese, English, French, Russian and Spanish texts are equally authentic, shall be deposited in the archives of the United Nations.

2. The Secretary-General of the United Nations shall transmit certified copies of the present Protocol to all States Parties to the Convention and all States that have signed the Convention.

OPTIONAL PROTOCOL TO THE CONVENTION ON THE RIGHTS OF THE CHILD ON THE INVOLVEMENT OF CHILDREN IN ARMED CONFLICT

(Adopted and opened for signature, ratification and accession by General Assembly resolution A/RES/54/263 of 25 May 2000 entry into force 12 February 2002)

The States Parties to the present Protocol,

Encouraged by the overwhelming support for the Convention on the Rights of the Child, demonstrating the widespread commitment that exists to strive for the promotion and protection of the rights of the child,

Reaffirming that the rights of children require special protection, and calling for continuous improvement of the situation of children without distinction, as well as for their development and education in conditions of peace and security,

Disturbed by the harmful and widespread impact of armed conflict on children and the long-term consequences it has for durable peace, security and development,

Condemning the targeting of children in situations of armed conflict and direct attacks on objects protected under international law, including places that generally have a significant presence of children, such as schools and hospitals,

Noting the adoption of the Rome Statute of the International Criminal Court, in particular, the inclusion therein as a war crime, of conscripting or enlisting children under the age of 15 years or using them to participate actively in hostilities in both international and non-international armed conflicts,

Considering therefore that to strengthen further the implementation of rights recognized in the Convention on the Rights of the Child there is a need to increase the protection of children from involvement in armed conflict,

Noting that article 1 of the Convention on the Rights of the Child specifies that, for the purposes of that Convention, a child means every human being below the age of 18 years unless, under the law applicable to the child, majority is attained earlier,

Convinced that an optional protocol to the Convention that raises the age of possible recruitment of persons into armed forces and their participation in hostilities will contribute effectively to the implementation of the principle that the best interests of the child are to be a primary consideration in all actions concerning children,

Noting that the twenty-sixth International Conference of the Red Cross and Red Crescent in December 1995 recommended, inter alia, that parties to conflict take every feasible step to ensure that children below the age of 18 years do not take part in hostilities,

Welcoming the unanimous adoption, in June 1999, of International Labour Organization Convention No. 182 on the Prohibition and Immediate Action for the Elimination of the Worst Forms of Child Labour, which prohibits, inter alia, forced or compulsory recruitment of children for use in armed conflict,

Condemning with the gravest concern the recruitment, training and use within and across national borders of children in hostilities by armed groups distinct from the armed forces of a State, and recognizing the responsibility of those who recruit, train and use children in this regard,

Recalling the obligation of each party to an armed conflict to abide by the provisions of international humanitarian law,

Stressing that the present Protocol is without prejudice to the purposes and principles contained in the Charter of the United Nations, including Article 51, and relevant norms of humanitarian law,

Bearing in mind that conditions of peace and security based on full respect of the purposes and principles contained in the Charter and observance of applicable human rights instruments are indispensable for the full protection of children, in particular during armed conflicts and foreign occupation,

Recognizing the special needs of those children who are particularly vulnerable to recruitment or use in hostilities contrary to the present Protocol owing to their economic or social status or gender,

Mindful of the necessity of taking into consideration the economic, social and political root causes of the involvement of children in armed conflicts,

Convinced of the need to strengthen international cooperation in the implementation of the present Protocol, as well as the physical and psychosocial rehabilitation and social reintegration of children who are victims of armed conflict,

Encouraging the participation of the community and, in particular, children and child victims in the dissemination of informational and educational programmes concerning the implementation of the Protocol,

Have agreed as follows:

Article 1

States Parties shall take all feasible measures to ensure that members of their armed forces who have not attained the age of 18 years do not take a direct part in hostilities.

Article 2

States Parties shall ensure that persons who have not attained the age of 18 years are not compulsorily recruited into their armed forces.

Article 3

1. States Parties shall raise in years the minimum age for the voluntary recruitment of persons into their national armed forces from that set out in article 38, paragraph 3, of the Convention on the Rights of the Child, taking account of the principles contained in that article and recognizing that under the Convention persons under the age of 18 years are entitled to special protection.

2. Each State Party shall deposit a binding declaration upon ratification of or accession to the present Protocol that sets forth the minimum age at which it will permit voluntary recruitment into its national armed forces and a description of the safeguards it has adopted to ensure that such recruitment is not forced or coerced.

3. States Parties that permit voluntary recruitment into their national armed forces under the age of 18 years shall maintain safeguards to ensure, as a minimum, that:

(a) Such recruitment is genuinely voluntary;

(b) Such recruitment is carried out with the informed consent of the person's parents or legal guardians;

(c) Such persons are fully informed of the duties involved in such military service;

(d) Such persons provide reliable proof of age prior to acceptance into national military service.

4. Each State Party may strengthen its declaration at any time by notification to that effect addressed to the Secretary-General of the United Nations, who shall inform all States Parties. Such notification shall take effect on the date on which it is received by the Secretary-General.

5. The requirement to raise the age in paragraph 1 of the present article does not apply to schools operated by or under the control of the armed

forces of the States Parties, in keeping with articles 28 and 29 of the Convention on the Rights of the Child.

Article 4

1. Armed groups that are distinct from the armed forces of a State should not, under any circumstances, recruit or use in hostilities persons under the age of 18 years.

2. States Parties shall take all feasible measures to prevent such recruitment and use, including the adoption of legal measures necessary to prohibit and criminalize such practices.

3. The application of the present article shall not affect the legal status of any party to an armed conflict.

Article 5

Nothing in the present Protocol shall be construed as precluding provisions in the law of a State Party or in international instruments and international humanitarian law that are more conducive to the realization of the rights of the child.

Article 6

1. Each State Party shall take all necessary legal, administrative and other measures to ensure the effective implementation and enforcement of the provisions of the present Protocol within its jurisdiction.

2. States Parties undertake to make the principles and provisions of the present Protocol widely known and promoted by appropriate means, to adults and children alike.

3. States Parties shall take all feasible measures to ensure that persons within their jurisdiction recruited or used in hostilities contrary to the present Protocol are demobilized or otherwise released from service. States Parties shall, when necessary, accord to such persons all appropriate assistance for their physical and psychological recovery and their social reintegration.

Article 7

1. States Parties shall cooperate in the implementation of the present Protocol, including in the prevention of any activity contrary thereto and in the rehabilitation and social reintegration of persons who are victims of acts contrary thereto, including through technical cooperation and financial assistance. Such assistance and cooperation will be undertaken in consultation with the States Parties concerned and the relevant international organizations.

2. States Parties in a position to do so shall provide such assistance through existing multilateral, bilateral or other programmes or, inter alia, through a voluntary fund established in accordance with the rules of the General Assembly.

Article 8

1. Each State Party shall, within two years following the entry into force of the present Protocol for that State Party, submit a report to the Committee on the Rights of the Child providing comprehensive information on the measures it has taken to implement the provisions of the Protocol, including the measures taken to implement the provisions on participation and recruitment.

2. Following the submission of the comprehensive report, each State Party shall include in the reports it submits to the Committee on the Rights of the Child, in accordance with article 44 of the Convention, any further information with respect to the implementation of the Protocol. Other States Parties to the Protocol shall submit a report every five years.

3. The Committee on the Rights of the Child may request from States Parties further information relevant to the implementation of the present Protocol.

Article 9

1. The present Protocol is open for signature by any State that is a party to the Convention or has signed it.

2. The present Protocol is subject to ratification and is open to accession by any State. Instruments of ratification or accession shall be deposited with the Secretary-General of the United Nations.

3. The Secretary-General, in his capacity as depositary of the Convention and the Protocol, shall inform all States Parties to the Convention and all States that have signed the Convention of each instrument of declaration pursuant to article 3.

Article 10

1. The present Protocol shall enter into force three months after the deposit of the tenth instrument of ratification or accession.

2. For each State ratifying the present Protocol or acceding to it after its entry into force, the Protocol shall enter into force one month after the date of the deposit of its own instrument of ratification or accession.

Article 11

1. Any State Party may denounce the present Protocol at any time by written notification to the Secretary- General of the United Nations, who shall thereafter inform the other States Parties to the Convention and all States that have signed the Convention. The denunciation shall take effect one year after the date of receipt of the notification by the Secretary-General. If, however, on the expiry of that year the denouncing State Party is engaged in armed conflict, the denunciation shall not take effect before the end of the armed conflict.

2. Such a denunciation shall not have the effect of releasing the State Party from its obligations under the present Protocol in regard to any act that occurs prior to the date on which the denunciation becomes effective. Nor shall such a denunciation prejudice in any way the continued consideration of any matter that is already under consideration by the Committee on the Rights of the Child prior to the date on which the denunciation becomes effective.

Article 12

1. Any State Party may propose an amendment and file it with the Secretary-General of the United Nations. The Secretary-General shall thereupon communicate the proposed amendment to States Parties with a request that they indicate whether they favour a conference of States Parties for the purpose of considering and voting upon the proposals. In the event that, within four months from the date of such communication, at least one third of the States Parties favour such a conference, the Secretary-General shall convene the conference under the auspices of the United Nations. Any amendment adopted by a majority of States Parties present and voting at the conference shall be submitted to the General Assembly of the United Nations for approval.

2. An amendment adopted in accordance with paragraph 1 of the present article shall enter into force when it has been approved by the General Assembly and accepted by a two-thirds majority of States Parties.

3. When an amendment enters into force, it shall be binding on those States Parties that have accepted it, other States Parties still being bound by the provisions of the present Protocol and any earlier amendments they have accepted.

Article 13

1. The present Protocol, of which the Arabic, Chinese, English, French, Russian and Spanish texts are equally authentic, shall be deposited in the archives of the United Nations.

2. The Secretary-General of the United Nations shall transmit certified copies of the present Protocol to all States Parties to the Convention and all States that have signed the Convention.

BRIDGING THE GAP—SUPPORT STRATEGY FOR CHILDREN AFFECTED BY ARMED CONFLICT

5th Ministerial Meeting of the Human Security Network Graz, 8 -10 May 2003

STATEMENTS

Preamble

We, Members of the Human Security Network, agree to give priority attention to the promotion and protection of the rights of children affected by armed conflict and therefore commit ourselves to a 'HSN Support Strategy' in this field. Action will be sought in preventing child rights violations and assisting child victims of armed conflict.

This political commitment is inspired by the overall imperative of bridging the gap between universal human rights standards and their implementation, between information and action and between programmatic concepts and systematic response on the ground. In line with the UN Secretary General's dictum of a general move to an 'era of application' in his report on Children and Armed Conflict, the present key elements have been identified as priority areas for strategic intervention by HSN Members.

By engaging in those core issues the Network seeks to add value to the international response to such situations in an action-oriented manner. Such added value is also demonstrated in combining the human rights based approach of the Network with its people centred human security perspective.

Important progress has already been achieved concerning the status of child rights evidenced by the near universal ratification of the Convention on the Rights of the Child (CRC), the entry into force of the Optional Protocol to the CRC on the involvement of Children in Armed Conflict and of the Optional Protocol to the CRC on the Sale of Children, Child

Prostitution, and Child Pornography. Such progress of standard set-ting has been complemented by the adoption of Security Council resolutions 1261(1999), 1314(2000), 1379(2001), 1460(2003) and the Plan of Action of the 2002 Special Session on Children of the General Assembly entitled "A World Fit for Children". This is the firm basis for HSN Members to launch this initiative.

HSN Members that have not yet done so will endeavour signing and ratifying or acceding to the relevant child rights instruments, in particular the Optional Protocols to the CRC, as they are essential for the implementation of this Strategy.

Founded upon the comprehensive standards of CRC and its general principles—the best interest of the child, the right to survival and development, the right to participation and to non-discrimination—HSN members will build upon research, advocacy and ongoing policy formulation, undertaken within the United Nations, regional organisations and by the many NGOs, both international and national. In this respect, HSN Members will support awareness building, programmatic interventions and other implementation efforts as well as continue and deepen their own programmes in the field.

All actions shall be taken either on behalf of HSN by the HSN Chair and/or individually by HSN members upon consultation.

Strengthening, monitoring and reporting

1. HSN members will give priority attention to the implementation by parties to armed conflict of their international obligations in respect of children. HSN will build these efforts on all applicable human rights standards, especially CRC and its Optional Protocols, international humanitarian law, international labour law, especially ILO Convention No. 182 on the Worst Forms of Child Labour, refugee law and the Guiding Principles on Internal Displacement.
2. To this end, HSN will
   - o support existing monitoring and reporting on violations of child rights by the United Nations system and other regional arrangements, especially field presences, Special Rapporteurs and Representatives as well as by the Committee on the Rights of the Child, NGOs and local child protection capacities.
   - o engage in information sharing, coordination of existing efforts and active co-operation with all relevant agencies and institutions, organisations on the regional and sub-regional

level such as the EU, OSCE, the African Union, the Organization of American States, ECOWAS, local actors, as well as the ICC.

- o call for more effective response mechanisms and more systematic operational activities with regard to monitoring and reporting.
- o promote advocacy and mainstreaming of the issue of child rights into the work of the deliberative organs/governing bodies of relevant international and regional organisations, UN treaty body and special procedures systems, decision making proc-esses and operational activities.

3. In doing so, the HSN will consult closely with specialised NGOs, research and think tank institutions benefiting from their important role and expertise in this field, and civil society at large. HSN Members will consider assuming responsibility for networking and assessing information in their respective regions including at the local level.

Focusing on Training activities

4. As a concrete contribution to improved monitoring and reporting HSN has developed a model curriculum for child rights/child protection training, child rights monitoring and child rehabilitation. On the basis of this general guide HSN members will consider starting to in-troduce specific child focused training for field staff engaged in missions organised bilater-ally, regionally or in cooperation with international organisations.
5. Such training echoing substantially the prevention aspect of the Support Strategy should be provided to all relevant categories of civil and military staff working in conflict and post conflict societies and adapted according to their specific functions.

Alarm function in response to child rights violations

6. HSN will aim at effecting an 'alarm function' in response to child rights violations in emerging, ongoing and post conflict situations with a view to bridging gaps—gaps between information and action as well as gaps between obligations/commitments and compliance. This may concern programmatic or institutional aspects as well as the level of interest regarding emerging, ongoing and post conflict situations. Specific attention will be given to particularly vulnerable groups of children.

7. With regard to information, monitoring and reporting HSN will base itself on the UNSG's list, SRSG/CAAC, UNICEF, UNHCR, OCHA, UN field presences, CHR Special Rapporteurs and Representatives, regional organisations, institutions like the ICC and specialised NGOs active on these issues. It will also make use of information and analysis gathered from representations of HSN members. At the regional level, the respective HSN Members will be attentive to situations giving rise to concern and signal cases to the Chair which might subsequently be taken up by the Network.
8. HSN Members will use their collective political weight, as appropriate, at national, regional and international levels to concretely address reported child rights violations upon consultation. Possible instruments for response include quiet diplomacy, demarches, statements and resolutions in relevant international fora and, if necessary, alerting media and public opinion in order to foster support for action at the political level.

Fighting impunity

9. HSN members underscore the importance of ensuring that there is no impunity for child rights violations and crimes against children. HSN members will work together to ensure that international and national justice and truth-seeking mechanisms during and after conflict address crimes against children and develop child sensitive procedures.
10. Concerning the International Criminal Court, HSN members will pay particular attention to the application of the specific provisions of the Rome Statute concerning children, and to the composition of the Court, thereby ensuring that a sufficient proportion of candidates for judicial and other positions have expertise in child rights.
11. HSN members will also promote the child specific aspects of accountability mechanisms (e.g. Sierra Leone, East Timor, Burundi, Cambodia). HSN Members that are already involved in the conflict resolution of specific countries/conflict situations will ensure that child rights issues are taken into account in the respective peace processes.
12. HSN members will ensure that criminal proceedings involving children affected by armed conflict are held in full respect of all guarantees and safeguards regarding juvenile justice. HSN Members will continue efforts to strengthen juvenile justice systems.

Focusing on protection of children with special needs, in particular girls

13. Based on the recommendations contained in the 2002 reports of the UNSG concerning children and armed conflict as well as women, peace and security, HSN will give priority attention to the protection of children with special needs, in particular the different needs of girls and boys, internally displaced children, sexually exploited children, children affected by HIV/AIDS and other STDs, unaccompanied children or child combatants.
14. On the basis of the Six Core Principles of the Inter-Agency Standing Committee on Emergencies HSN will givė special attention to the prevention of sexual exploitation and abuse against children, especially girls including female adolescents, and of sexually transmitted diseases including HIV/AIDS.
15. HSN will also support efforts aimed at promoting gender equality and at improving the capacity of girls to make their own decisions.
16. HSN Members will strive to enhance the protection of and assistance to internally displaced children in accordance with the Guiding Principles on Internal Displacement.
17. HSN Members will provide assistance to children disabled by landmines and of war-related injuries.

Promoting child participation in peace processes and post-conflict situations

18. Emphasis will be placed on the role children can play in the building of durable peace and in creating more equitable societies in the aftermath of conflicts. HSN will strive for their participation in the prevention and peaceful resolution of conflicts as well as in post conflict peace building processes.
19. Special attention needs to be given to appropriately include them in all demobilization, disarmament, rehabilitation, reintegration and post-conflict reconstruction programmes.
20. In addressing the problems and needs of children affected by armed conflict, the HSN will work for the inclusion of former child combatants in all programmes.

RIGHT TO DEVELOPMENT

Defining Development

We can define human development as expanding the choices for all people in society. There are four aspects to sustainable human development—all affecting the lives of the poor and vulnerable:

Empowerment—The expansion of men and women's capabilities and choices increases their ability to exercise those choices free of hunger, want and deprivation. It also increases their opportunity to participate in, or endorse, decision-making affecting their lives.

Co-operation—With a sense of belonging important for personal fulfillment, well-being and a sense of purpose and meaning, human development is concerned with the ways in which people work together and interact.

Equity—The expansion of capabilities and opportunities means more than income—it also means equity, such as an educational system to which everybody should have access.

Sustainability—The needs of this generation must be met without compromising the right of future generations to be free of poverty and deprivation and to exercise their basic capabilities- Particularly the security of livelihood. People need to be freed from threats, such as disease or repression and from sudden harmful disruptions in their lives.

The right to development is different from other kinds of rights. It does not belong only to individuals, but also to states. It is not justifiable, being in the nature of principles rather than substantive entitlements. The right is based on a resolution of the General Assembly, the Declaration on the Right to Development (1986). It is possible that a further work proceeds on it towards a more binding instrument, many of the points that are ambiguous or obscure will be clarified. At the present time the importance of this right is largely political.

If the scope and the ingredients of the rights could be clarified, and substantial agreement reached on them, it is possible that the right could play a valuable role by providing a basis for reconciling different kinds of rights and indicating a way towards their realisation. It is also valuable in providing a broad definition of development, moving away from narrow economic criteria to a more holistic view in which the participation of the people and their political and cultural development are emphasised.

The Declaration asserts rather defines the right to development, although the preamble proclaims that "development is a comprehensive economic, social cultural and political process, which aims at the constant improvement of the well being of the entire population and of all individuals on the basis of their active, free and meaningful participation in development and in the fair distribution of benefits there from". It states that the right to development is an inalienable human right whereby all human beings and all peoples are entitled to participate in, contribute to and enjoy economic, social, cultural and political development, in which all human rights and freedoms can be fully realized.

All human rights and fundamental freedoms are indivisible and should be equally implemented. The human being is the central subject of development and should be an active participant and beneficiary of the right to development. It is the state which has the primary responsibility for development. Poorer states should be helped by the richer to promote their development and a new international economic order should be established. The call for greater international co-operation is counter-balanced by the emphasis on national sovereignty.

One needs to be on guard that the Declaration is not used by governments as a further excuse to erode the autonomy of civil society or the rights of individuals or groups. It will also be necessary to resolve conflicts between this right, which encourages the full utilisation of natural resources with the right to a safe healthy environment and the preservation of resources for generations to come.

"Human rights and sustainable human development are inextricably linked" (UNDP 1998) only by definitional legerdemain. "Sustainable human development" simply redefines human rights, along with democracy, peace, and justice, as subsets of development. Aside from the fact that few ordinary people or governments use the term in this way, such a definition leaves un addressed the relationship between human rights and *economic* development, an important domain of contemporary social action and aspiration. Real tensions between these objectives cannot be evaded by stipulate definitions.

Declaration on the Right to Development

(Adopted by General Assembly resolution 41/128 of 4 December 1986)

The General Assembly,

Bearing in mind the purposes and principles of the Charter of the United Nations relating to the achievement of international co-operation in solving international problems of an economic, social, cultural or humanitarian nature, and in promoting and encouraging respect for human rights and fundamental freedoms for all without distinction as to race, sex, language or religion,

Recognizing that development is a comprehensive economic, social, cultural and political process, which aims at the constant improvement of the well-being of the entire population and of all individuals on the basis of their active, free and meaningful participation in development and in the fair distribution of benefits resulting there from,

Considering that under the provisions of the Universal Declaration of Human Rights everyone is entitled to a social and international order in which the rights and freedoms set forth in that Declaration can be fully realized,

Recalling the provisions of the International Covenant on Economic, Social and Cultural Rights and of the International Covenant on Civil and Political Rights,

Recalling further the relevant agreements, conventions, resolutions, recommendations and other instruments of the United Nations and its specialized agencies concerning the integral development of the human being, economic and social progress and development of all peoples, including those instruments concerning decolonization, the prevention of discrimination, respect for and observance of human rights and fundamental freedoms, the maintenance of international peace and security and the further promotion of friendly relations and co-operation among States in accordance with the Charter,

Recalling the right of peoples to self-determination, by virtue of which they have the right freely to determine their political status and to pursue their economic, social and cultural development,

Recalling also the right of peoples to exercise, subject to the relevant provisions of both International Covenants on Human Rights, full and complete sovereignty over all their natural wealth and resources,

Mindful of the obligation of States under the Charter to promote universal respect for and observance of human rights and fundamental freedoms for all without distinction of any kind such as race, colour, sex, language, religion, political or other opinion, national or social origin, property, birth or other status,

Considering that the elimination of the massive and flagrant violations of the human rights of the peoples and individuals affected by situations such as those resulting from colonialism, neo-colonialism, apartheid, all forms of racism and racial discrimination, foreign domination and occupation, aggression and threats against national sovereignty, national unity and territorial integrity and threats of war would contribute to the establishment of circumstances propitious to the development of a great part of mankind,

Concerned at the existence of serious obstacles to development, as well as to the complete fulfilment of human beings and of peoples, constituted, inter alia, by the denial of civil, political, economic, social and cultural rights, and considering that all human rights and fundamental freedoms are indivisible and interdependent and that, in order to promote development, equal attention and urgent consideration should be given to the implementation, promotion and protection of civil, political, economic, social and cultural rights and that, accordingly, the promotion of, respect for and enjoyment of certain human rights and fundamental freedoms cannot justify the denial of other human rights and fundamental freedoms,

Considering that international peace and security are essential elements for the realization of the right to development,

Reaffirming that there is a close relationship between disarmament and development and that progress in the field of disarmament would considerably promote progress in the field of development and that resources released through disarmament measures should be devoted to the economic and social development and well-being of all peoples and, in particular, those of the developing countries,

Recognizing that the human person is the central subject of the development process and that development policy should therefore make the human being the main participant and beneficiary of development,

Recognizing that the creation of conditions favourable to the development of peoples and individuals is the primary responsibility of their States,

Aware that efforts at the international level to promote and protect human rights should be accompanied by efforts to establish a new international economic order,

Confirming that the right to development is an inalienable human right and that equality of opportunity for development is a prerogative both of nations and of individuals who make up nations,

Proclaims the following Declaration on the Right to Development:

Article 1

1. The right to development is an inalienable human right by virtue of which every human person and all peoples are entitled to participate in, contribute to, and enjoy economic, social, cultural and political development, in which all human rights and fundamental freedoms can be fully realized.

2. The human right to development also implies the full realization of the right of peoples to self-determination, which includes, subject to the relevant provisions of both International Covenants on Human Rights, the exercise of their inalienable right to full sovereignty over all their natural wealth and resources.

Article 2

1. The human person is the central subject of development and should be the active participant and beneficiary of the right to development.

2. All human beings have a responsibility for development, individually and collectively, taking into account the need for full respect for their human rights and fundamental freedoms as well as their duties to the community, which alone can ensure the free and complete fulfilment of the human being, and they should therefore promote and protect an appropriate political, social and economic order for development.

3. States have the right and the duty to formulate appropriate national development policies that aim at the constant improvement of the well-being of the entire population and of all individuals, on the basis of their active, free and meaningful participation in development and in the fair distribution of the benefits resulting therefrom.

Article 3

1. States have the primary responsibility for the creation of national and international conditions favourable to the realization of the right to development.

2. The realization of the right to development requires full respect for the principles of international law concerning friendly relations and co-operation among States in accordance with the Charter of the United Nations.

3. States have the duty to co-operate with each other in ensuring development and eliminating obstacles to development. States should realize their rights and fulfil their duties in such a manner as to promote a new international economic order based on sovereign equality, interdependence, mutual interest and co-operation among all States, as well as to encourage the observance and realization of human rights.

Article 4

1. States have the duty to take steps, individually and collectively, to formulate international development policies with a view to facilitating the full realization of the right to development.

2. Sustained action is required to promote more rapid development of developing countries. As a complement to the efforts of developing countries, effective international co-operation is essential in providing these countries with appropriate means and facilities to foster their comprehensive development.

Article 5

States shall take resolute steps to eliminate the massive and flagrant violations of the human rights of peoples and human beings affected by situations such as those resulting from apartheid, all forms of racism and racial discrimination, colonialism, foreign domination and occupation, aggression, foreign interference and threats against national sovereignty, national unity and territorial integrity, threats of war and refusal to recognize the fundamental right of peoples to self-determination.

Article 6

1. All States should co-operate with a view to promoting, encouraging and strengthening universal respect for and observance of all human rights and fundamental freedoms for all without any distinction as to race, sex, language or religion.

2. All human rights and fundamental freedoms are indivisible and interdependent; equal attention and urgent consideration should be given to the implementation, promotion and protection of civil, political, economic, social and cultural rights.

3. States should take steps to eliminate obstacles to development resulting from failure to observe civil and political rights, as well as economic social and cultural rights.

Article 7

All States should promote the establishment, maintenance and strengthening of international peace and security and, to that end, should do their utmost to achieve general and complete disarmament under effective international control, as well as to ensure that the resources released by effective disarmament measures are used for comprehensive development, in particular that of the developing countries.

Article 8

1. States should undertake, at the national level, all necessary measures for the realization of the right to development and shall ensure, inter alia, equality of opportunity for all in their access to basic resources, education, health services, food, housing, employment and the fair distribution of income. Effective measures should be undertaken to ensure that women have an active role in the development process. Appropriate economic and social reforms should be carried out with a view to eradicating all social injustices.

2. States should encourage popular participation in all spheres as an important factor in development and in the full realization of all human rights.

Article 9

1. All the aspects of the right to development set forth in the present Declaration are indivisible and interdependent and each of them should be considered in the context of the whole.

2. Nothing in the present Declaration shall be construed as being contrary to the purposes and principles of the United Nations, or as implying that any State, group or person has a right to engage in any activity or to perform any act aimed at the violation of the rights set forth in the Universal Declaration of Human Rights and in the International Covenants on Human Rights.

Article 10

Steps should be taken to ensure the full exercise and progressive enhancement of the right to development, including the formulation, adoption and implementation of policy, legislative and other measures at the national and international levels.

INTELLECTUAL PROPERTY RIGHTS

Meaning

Intellectual Property Rights (IPR) is a general term covering patents, copyright, trademark, industrial designs, geographical indications, protection of layout design of integrated circuits and protection of undisclosed information (trade secrets).

Intellectual property rights in India

As was the case with China, India too showed signs of resistance to quick enforcement of international intellectual property right (IPR) protection laws as demanded by the developed countries, particularly the US. China could get away on grounds that it is not a member of the World Trade Organisation (WTO), but India was required to comply. Under the terms of the WTO, India is required to implement WTO-standard IPR protection laws by 2005. It must be acknowledged that there has been remarkable progress in IPR protection in the field of software and cinema products.

However, under pressure from its own domestic industry and the United States, India strengthened its copyright law in May 1994, placing it at par with international practice. The new law, which entered into force in May, 1995, fully reflects the provisions of the Berne Convention on copyrights, to which India is a party. Based on its improved copyright protection, India's designation as a "priority foreign country" under the United States' Special-301 list was revoked and India was placed on the "priority watch list." Copyright enforcement is also rapidly improving.

Classification of copyright infringements as "cognisable offenses" expands police search and seizure authority. While the formation of appellate boards under the new legislation should speed prosecution, local attorneys indicate that some technical flaws in the laws, which require administrative approval prior to police action, need to be corrected.

Trademark protection is considered good by the US authorities, and could be raised to international standards with the passage of a new trademark bill that codifies existing court decisions on the use and protection of foreign trademarks, including service marks. The bill was first introduced in 1995 but failed to win parliamentary approval. Passage of the trademark bill is expected in 1998. Enforcement of trademark owner rights had been weak in the past, but is steadily improving as the courts and police respond to domestic concerns about the high cost of piracy to Indian rights' holders.

India's patent act prohibits product patents for any invention intended for use or capable of being used as a food, medicine, or drug or relating to substances prepared or produced by chemical processes. Consequently, many drugs invented by foreign companies are widely reproduced.

Processes for making drugs are patentable, but the patent term is limited to the shorter of five years from the grant of patent or seven years from the filing date of the patent application. Product patents in other areas are granted for 14 years from the date of filing. However, as a signatory to the Uruguay Round of GATT, including its provisions on Trade- Related Intellectual Property Rights (TRIPS), India must introduce a comprehensive system of product patents no later than 2005.

The Indian government has formed an advisory committee to recommend changes in the 1970 Indian Patents Act. A temporary ordinance for patent protection implementing the "mailbox" provisions of the WTO TRIPS agreement and providing for exclusive marketing rights was issued in December 1994. However, the ordinance lapsed and the parliament has yet to pass a new patent bill implementing the provisions of the ordinance.

In July 1996, the U.S. initiated WTO dispute settlement procedures over India's failure to implement its TRIPS obligations. The final panel report on this case was issued in August 1997, and ruled that India had failed to meet its obligations under the TRIPS agreement.

PATENT

A patent is an exclusive right granted by a country to the owner of an invention to make, use, manufacture and market the invention, provided the invention satisfies certain conditions stipulated in the law. Exclusivity of right implies that no one else can make, use, manufacture or market the invention without the consent of the patent holder. This right is available only for a limited period of time. However, the use or exploitation of a patent may be affected by other laws of the country which has awarded the patent.

These laws may relate to health, safety, food, security etc. Further, existing patents in similar area may also come in the way. A patent in the law is a property right and hence, can be gifted, inherited, assigned, sold or licensed. As the right is conferred by the State, it can be revoked by the State under very special circumstances even if the patent has been sold or licensed or manufactured or marketed in the meantime. The patent right is territorial in nature and inventors/their assignees will have to file separate patent applications in countries of their interest, along with necessary fees, for obtaining patents in those countries.

A patentee must disclose the invention in a patent document for anyone to practice it after the expiry of the patent or practice it with the consent of the patent holder during the life of the patent.

Conditions to be satisfied by an invention to be patentable

An invention must satisfy the following three conditions :

(*i*) *Novelty* : An invention will be considered novel if it does not form a part of the global state of the art. Information appearing in magazines, technical journals, books, newspapers etc. constitute the state of the art. Oral description of the invention in a seminar/conference can also spoil novelty. Novelty is assessed in a global context. An invention will cease to be novel if it has been disclosed in the public through any type of publications anywhere in the world before filing a patent application in respect of the invention. Prior use of the invention in the country of interest before the filing date can also destroy the novelty. Novelty is determined through extensive literature and patent searches. It should be realized that patent search is essential and critical for ascertaining novelty as most of the information reported in patent documents does not get published any where else.

(*ii*) *Inventiveness (Non-obviousness)* : A patent application involves an inventive step if the proposed invention is not obvious to a person skilled in the art i.e., skilled in the subject matter of the patent application. The prior art should not point towards the invention implying that the practitioner of the subject matter could not have thought about the invention prior to filing of the patent application. Inventiveness cannot be decided on the material contained in unpublished patents. The complexity or the simplicity of an inventive step does not have any bearing on the grant of a patent. In other words a very simple invention can qualify for a patent. If there is an inventive step between the proposed patent and the prior art at that point of time, then an invention has taken place. A mere 'scintilla' of invention is sufficient to found a valid patent.

(*iii*) *Usefulness:* An invention must possess utility for the grant of patent. No valid patent can be granted for an invention devoid of utility.

Patentable inventions under the Patents Act, 1970

Invention means any new and useful

(a) Art, process, method or manner of manufacture

(b) Machine, apparatus or other article

(c) Substances produced by manufacture, and include any new and useful improvements of any of them and an alleged invention.

However, inventions claiming substance intended for use, or capable of being used, as food or as medicine or drug or relating to substances prepared or produced by chemical processes (including alloys, optical glass, semiconductors and inter-metallic compounds) are not patentable.

Types of inventions which are not patentable in India

An invention may satisfy the conditions of novelty, inventiveness and usefulness but it may not qualify for a patent under the following situations:

(*i*) An invention which is frivolous or which claims anything obviously contrary to well established natural laws e.g. different types of perpetual motion machines.

(*ii*) An invention the primary or intended use of which would be contrary to law or morality or injurious to public health e.g. a process for the preparation of a beverage which involves use of a carcinogenic substance, although the beverage may have higher nourishment value.

(*iii*) The mere discovery of a scientific principles or formulation of an abstract theory e.g., Raman effect.

(*iv*) The mere discovery of any new property or new use of known substance or the mere use of a known process, machine or apparatus unless such a known process results in a new product or employs at least one new reactant.

(*v*) A substance obtained by a mere admixture resulting only in the aggregation of the properties of the components thereof or a process for producing such substance.

(*vi*) The mere arrangement or rearrangement or duplication of features of known devices each functioning independently of one another in a known way.

(*vii*) A method or process of testing applicable during the process of manufacture for rendering the machine, apparatus or other equipment more efficient.

(*viii*) A method of agriculture or horticulture.

(*ix*) Any process for medical, surgical, curative, prophylactic or other treatment of human beings, or any process for a similar treatment of animals or plants.

(*x*) Inventions relating to atomic energy.

Filing of an Application for Patent

Filing of an application for a patent should be completed at the earliest possible date and should not be delayed. An application filed with provisional specification, disclosing the essence of the nature of the invention helps to register the priority by the applicant. Delay in filing an application may entail some risks like (i) other inventors might forestall the first inventor by applying for a patent for the said invention (ii) there may be either an inadvertent publication of the invention by the inventor himself/herself or by others independently of him/her.

Publication of an invention in any form by the inventor before filing of a patent application would disqualify the invention to be patentable. Hence, inventors should not disclose their inventions before filing the patent application. The invention should be considered for publication after a patent application has been filed. Thus, it can be seen that there is no contradiction between publishing an inventive work and filing of patent application in respect of the invention.

Date of Patent

The date of patent is the date of filing the complete specification. This is an important date because it is from this date that the legal protection of an invention covered in the patent takes effect. The term of the patent is counted from this date.

Term of a patent in the Indian system

(*a*) Five years from the date of sealing of the patent or seven years from the date of the patent (i. e. the date of filing the complete specification), whichever period is shorter, for an invention claiming the method or process of manufacture of a substance, where the substance is intended or capable of being used as a drug, medicine or food.

(*b*) Fourteen years from the date of patent in respect of any other patentable invention.

A patent has to be maintained by paying the maintenance fees every year. If the maintenance fees is not paid, the patent will cease to remain in force and the invention becomes open to public. Anyone can then utilize the patent without the danger of infringing the patent.

Essential patent documents to be generated and submitted

There are two types of patent documents usually known as patent specification, namely

(*i*) Provisional Specification and (*ii*) Complete Specification

(i) Provisional Specification

A provisional specification is usually filed to establish priority of the invention in case the disclosed invention is only at a conceptual stage and a delay is expected in submitting full and specific description of the invention. Although, a patent application accompanied with provisional specification does not confer any legal patent rights to the applicants, it is, however, a very important document to establish the earliest ownership of an invention.

The provisional specification is a permanent and independent scientific cum legal document and no amendment is allowed in this. No patent is granted on the basis of a provisional specification. It has to be followed by a complete specification for obtaining a patent for the said invention. Complete specification must be submitted within 12 months of filing the provisional specification. This period can be extended by 3 months. It is not necessary to file an application with provisional specification before the complete specification. An application with complete specification can be filed right at the first instance.

(ii) Complete Specification

Submission of complete specification is necessary to obtain a patent. The contents of a complete specification would include the following:

1. Title of the invention.
2. Field to which the invention belongs
3. Background of the invention including prior art giving drawbacks of the known inventions&practices.
4. Complete description of the invention along with experimental results.
5. Drawings etc.essential for understanding the invention.
6. Claims, which are statements, related to the invention on which legal proprietorship is being sought. Therefore the claims have to be drafted very carefully.

Criteria for naming inventors in an application for patent

The naming of inventors is normally decided on the basis of the following criteria:

(*i*) All persons who contribute towards development of patentable features of an invention should be named inventor(s).

(*ii*) All persons, who have made intellectual contribution in achieving the final results of the research work leading to a patent, should be named inventor(s).

(*iii*) A person who has not contributed intellectually in the development of an invention is not entitled to be included as an inventor.

(*iv*) A person who provides ideas needed to produce the 'germs of the invention' need not himself / herself carry out the experiments, constructs the apparatus with his/her own hands or make the drawings himself/herself. The person may take the help or others. Such person who have helped in conducting the experiments, constructing apparatus or making the drawings or models without providing any intellectual inputs are not entitled to be named inventors.

Quite often difficulties are experienced in deciding the names of inventors. To avoid such a situation, it is very essential that all scientists engaged in research should keep factual, clear and accurate recorded of daily work done by them in the form of diary. The pages in the diary should be consecutively numbered and the entries made be signed both by the scientists and the concerned leader.

Nature of information needed while consulting a patent attorney

As an inventor one should share the complete invention with a patent attorney in the same manner as a patient confides in a doctor. As a doctor may not be able to write a correct prescription without knowing the details of the disease/problem, a patent attorney may not be able to draft a good specification in the absence of details about the invention. Following points should be kept in mind while discussing with the attorney:

(*i*) Provide complete details of the invention including failures, if any, on the way to the invention.

Do not feel bad if attorney asks you questions like where did you get the idea from or did you copy the idea from somewhere or are you keeping other inventors working with you on the inventorship or have you published the invention or disclosed it in a seminar/conference or have you displayed the invention in an exhibition? A patent document is a techno-legal document, hence all precautions are to be taken right from the first step. Provides right answers and you may even show your laboratory note book/log book to the attorney. This will help the attorney / agent to explain the inventive step in a precise manner and draft a good specification and associated claims.

(*ii*) Explain the central theme of the invention and novelty, inventiveness and utility of the invention.

(*iii*) Share all the prior art documents in your possession with the attorney.

(*iv*) If you have developed an improved version of your competitor's product/process, admit it and be totally honest. This would help the attorney in drafting precise claims and avoid excessive claims, which might be struck down immediately or at a later date.

(*v*) A detailed description of the best way of putting the invention into practical use, results of your tests and trials, etc., including all failures and defects should be given to the attorney.

(*vi*) Alternative ways of using the invention, and the substitutes or parts of it i.e., will one chemical compound do as well as any other in the process?

(*vii*) It may be worth drafting the patent widely enough to cover less satisfactory alternatives as well so as to prevent rivals from marketing a less satisfactory competing product which because of its defects might bring the whole genre of product into disrepute or which may be cheap.

(*viii*) Both after an initial search and during the course of the filing and grant of a patent application, it is important to respond quickly and accurately to queries which the patent attorney may have. Thus the client should keep the patent attorney informed of any new develop-ments in the field of invention carried by the patentee or some one else.

Cost of filing a patent application in India

The Government fee for filing a patent application (complete/ provisional) in India is Rs. 1,500/- for individuals and Rs. 5,000/- for legal entities. A sealing fee of Rs. 1,500/- for individuals and Rs. 5,000/- for legal entities has to be paid at the time of grant (sealing) of patent.

Nature of Patent Rights

There is nothing like a global patent or a world patent. Patent rights are essentially territorial in nature and are protected only in a country (or countries) which,has (have) granted these rights. In other words,-for obtaining patent rights in different countries one has to submit patent applications in all the countries of interest for grant of patents. This would entail payment of official fees and associated expenses, like the attorney fees, essential for obtaining patent rights in each country. However, there are some regional systems where by filing one application one could simultaneously obtain patents in the member countries of a regional system; European Patent Office is an example of a similar system.

Each country is free to grant or refuse a patent on the bases of scrutiny by its patent office. This means that granting a patent in one country of the Union does not force other countries to grant the patent for the same invention. Also, the refusal of the patent in one country does not mean that it will be terminated in all the countries.

Paris Convention

The Paris Convention is an international convention for promoting trade among the member countries, devised to facilitate protection of industrial property simultaneously in the member countries without any loss in the priority date. All the member countries provide national treatment to all the applications from the other member countries for protection of industrial property rights. The Convention was first signed in 1883. Since then, the Convention has been revised several times, in 1900 at Brussels, in 1911 at Washington, in 1925 at the Hague, in 1934 at London, in 1958 at Lisbon and in 1967 at Stockholm.

Principal Features

***(i)* National treatment:** This is a very important concept and is essential for successfully achieving the fundamental aim of the Paris Convention. The idea is to provide equal treatment to applications from member countries, in a given member country and not to differentiate between the nationals of your country and nationals of the other countries for the purpose of grant, and protection of industrial property in your country. Imagine that a national of country X applies for grant of a patent in India. According to the Paris Convention, the Indian Patent Office shall apply the same norms and rules, to the applicant from X, as applicable to an Indian applicant, for granting a patent.

Similarly the applicant from X shall have the same protection after grant and identical legal remedies against any infringement shall be available to the applicant provided the conditions and formalities imposed upon Indians are complied with. No requirement as to domicile or establishment in the country where protection is claimed, may be imposed.

(*ii*) Right of priority: The date from which patent right is deemed to start is usually the date of filing of complete specification. To obtain rights in other member countries, the application must be filed on the same day in other member countries if it is desired to have the rights started from the same day. However, there are practical difficulties in synchronizing the activities.

For facilitating simultaneous protection in member countries, the Convention provides that within 12 months of national filing, if patent applications are filed in those member countries, the patents, if granted in member countries, will be effective from the date of national filing. This right is known as the right of priority. In other words you maintain the priority or the same date of filing in all the member countries and no one else in those countries can obtain the patent rights on a similar/identical invention from the same or a later date.

In case the applicant after a second look at the patent application finds that thé patent contains more than one invention or on his own accord wishes to divide the application, he can claim the initial date of priority for subsequent patent applications. The applicant may also, on his own initiative, divide a patent application and preserve as the date of each divisional application the date of the initial application and the benefit of the right of priority, if any. Each country of the Union shall have the right to determine the conditions under which such division shall be authorized.

(*iii*) Independence of patents

(*iv*) Parallel importation : Importation is considered as working of patent, provided the patented product is manufactured in a member country and is imported into another member country which has also granted a patent on the same invention to the same applicant. Imagine that a product X has been patented in two member countries A and B. The product X is then manufactured in country A and imported into the country B. This product X shall enjoy the same patent protection in the country B even though it has been manufactured in the country A. This would also be considered as if the patent has been worked in country B.

(*v*) Protection against false indications and unfair competition

Territorial nature of Patent rights: There is nothing like a global patent or a world patent. Patent rights are essentially territorial in nature and are protected only in a country (or countries) which has (have) granted these rights. In other words,-for obtaining patent rights in different countries one has to submit patent applications in all the countries of interest for grant of patents. This would entail payment of official fees and associated expenses, like the attorney fees, essential for obtaining patent rights in each country. However, there are some regional systems where by filing one application one could simultaneously obtain patents in the member countries of a regional system; European Patent Office is an example of a similar system.

Each country is free to grant or refuse a patent on the bases of scrutiny by its patent office. This means that granting a patent in one country of the Union does not force other countries to grant the patent for the same invention. Also, the refusal of the patent in one country does not mean that it will be terminated in all the countries.

Copyright : Copy right cover the following:

(*i*) Literary, dramatic and musical work. Computer programs/ software are covered within the definition of literary work.

(*ii*) Artistic work.

(*iii*) Cinematographic films which include sound track and video films.

(*iv*) Record-any disc, tape, perforated roll or other device.

Rights of a copyright holder

(*a*) In the case of literary, dramatic or musical work, not being a computer program——

(*i*) to reproduce the work in any material form including the storing of it in any medium by electronic means;

(*ii*) to issue copies of the work to the public not being copies already in circulation;

(*iii*) to perform the work in public, or communicate it to the public; to make any cinematography film or sound recording in respect of the work;

(*iv*) to make any translation of the work; to make any adaptation of the work;

(*v*) to do, in relation to a translation or an adaptation of the work, any of the acts specified in relation to the work in sub-clauses (i) to (vi);

(b) in the case of computer program -

(*i*) to do any acts specified in clauses (a);
(*ii*) to sell or give on hire, or offer for sale or hire any copy of
(*iii*) the computer program, regardless of whether such copy has been sold or given on hire on earlier occasions;

(c) in the case of an artistic work –

(*i*) to reproduce the work in any material form including depiction in three dimensions of a two dimensional work or in two dimensions of a three dimensional work;
(*ii*) to communicate the work to the public;
(*iii*) to issue copies of the work to the public not being copies already in circulation;
(*iv*) to include the work in any cinematography film.
(*v*) to make any adaptation of the work;
(*vi*) to do, in relation to a translation or an adaptation of the work, any of the acts specified in relation to the work in sub-clauses (i) to (vi);

(d) in the case of a cinematography film -

(*i*) to make a copy of the film including a photograph of. any image forming part thereof;
(*ii*) to sell or give on hire or offer for sale or hire, any copy of the film, regardless of whether such copy has been sold or given on hire on earlier occasions;
(*iii*) to communicate the film to the public; (e) in the case of sound recording -
(*iv*) to make any other sound recording embodying it;
(*v*) to sell or give on hire or offer for sale or hire, any copy of the,sound recording, regardless of whether such copy has been sold or given on hire on earlier occasions;
(*vi*) to communicate the sound recording to the public;

Terms of a copyright

(a) If published within the life time of the author of a literary work the term is for the life time of the author plus 60 years.

(b) For cinematography films, records, photographs, posthumous publications, anonymous' publication, works of government and international agencies the term is 60 years from the beginning of the calendar year following the year in which the work was published.

(c) For broadcasting the term is 25 years from the beginning of the calendar year following the year, in which the broadcast was made.

The rule for the transfer of copyright

The owner of the copyright in an existing work or prospective owner of the copyright in a future work may assign to any person the copyright, either wholly or partially in the following manner.

- for the entire world or for a specific country or territory; or
- for the full term of copyright or part thereof ; or
- relating to all the rights comprising the copyright or only part of such rights.

CONSUMER RIGHTS

Consumer- Definition

A Consumer is anyone who buys or agrees to buy any goods for a consideration which has been paid or promised or partly paid and partly promised or under any system of deferred payment, consumer also includes any user of such goods other than the person who actually buys goods and such use is made with the approval of the purchaser. However, a person is not a consumer if he/she purchases goods for commercial or resale purpose. But there are exceptions. For example a person is a consumer if he/she purchases goods for the purpose of earning his/her livelihood by means of self-employment. For example it has been held in the case where a lady purchased a photocopier for the sole purpose of earning her livelihood and not for large scale business or trading activity that it was not a commercial activity and she was considered a consumer (the secretary, Consumer Guidance & Research Society of India V. M/s. BPL India Ltd.–1 (1992) CPJ 140NC).

In the case of "services" a "consumer" means a person who hires or avails of any service or services for a consideration which has been paid or promised or partly paid and partly promised or under any system of deferred payment. It also includes any beneficiary of such service other than the one who actually hires or avails of the service for consideration and such services are availed with the approval of such person.

One of the most important milestones in the area of consumer protection in the country has been the enactment of the **Consumer Protection Act, 1986**. This Act has been necessitated since the well organized sectors of manufacturers, traders and service providers continued exploiting the consumers, despite the existence of various provisions of laws and the Civil Courts protecting their interest. The Consumer Protection Act, 1986, was enacted to fill the gap of an acute need to protect the interests of the consumers. This Act was further amended in 1993 introducing some very important provisions beneficial to the consumers.

The Consumer Protection Act, 1986 is a unique and comprehen-sive legislation. The objects and reasons behind the Act are based on **inherent rights.**

This Act has set in motion a revolution in the field of consumer rights, the parallel of which has not been seen anywhere else in the world.

What is a service?

The "service", in the Act, means service of any description which is made available to its potential users and includes provision of facilities in connection with banking, financing, insurance, transport, processing, supply of electrical or other energy, boarding or lodging or both, entertainment or amusement or the supply of news or other information. It is important to note that it does not include the rendering of any services free of charge or under a contract of personal service.

Under the Consumer Protection Act, a consumer can lodge complaints about his doctor, lawyer, tax consultant, tailor-master or any other services for which he has paid and feels that he has not been given his due. In all these matters the grievances of the consumers have been attended and the consumer forums in different parts of the country have issued suitable directions.

For example, Education is a service within the purview of the Act.

Unlike existing laws which are punitive or preventive in nature, the provisions of this Act are compensatory in nature. The Act is intended to provide simple, speedy and inexpensive redressal to the consumers' grievances and relief of a specific nature and award of compensation wherever appropriate to the consumer.

Consumer Rights

1. ***Right to safety.*** It is the right to be protected against the marketing of goods and services that are hazardous to life and property. So one should be cautious in purchasing goods and services. The consumer should be aware of purchasing goods not marked with **ISI** or **AGMARK** and in case of absence of such marks should inquire from the shopkeeper about the quality of the goods.

2. ***Right to be informed.*** The consumer has a right to be informed about the quality, quantity, potency, purity, standard, and price of goods so as to protect himself against unfair trade practice.

3. ***Right to choose.*** The right to be assured, whenever possible, to access the authority of goods and services at competitive prices. It means access of the consumer to a wide variety of goods at competitive prices.

4. ***Right to be heard and assured*** It means that the consumers' interests will receive due consideration at appropriate forums. There should be appropriate forum for a consumer to approach in case he feels cheated or duped.

5. ***Right to seek redressal.*** The consumer has a right to seek redressal against unfair trade practices or unscrupulous exploitations. The consumer could take up the matter with the offending party. If there is no redressal he can take up the matter with the consumer association in the area.

6. ***Right to consumer education.*** The consumer organizations can play a constructive role in consumer education. They can inform the consumer about their rights and also teach them how to seek, use, and evaluate consumer information. The need for such an action is more acute in the rural areas.

The Central and State Consumers Protection Councils are to be protected and promoted the above objectives.

Relief available to consumers

The Act provides for simple, speedy and inexpensive redressal of grievances and is compensatory in nature. There is no complexities or technicalities involved, even there is no court fee or stamp duty to be affixed, no matter whatever be the amount involved in the complaints.

Based on these rights, reliefs are available to a consumer which is depending on the nature of relief sought by the consumer and facts, the Redressal Forums may give orders for one or more of the following reliefs

1. replacement of the goods,
2. removal of defects from the goods,
3. refund of the price paid,
4. removal of defects in the goods or deficiencies in the services,
5. award of compensation for the loss or injury suffered,
6. discontinuance of unfair trade practices or restrictive trade practices or direction not to repeat them,
7. not to offer the hazardous goods for sale,

8. award for adequate costs to parties or
9. withdrawal of the hazardous goods from being offered to sale

Consumer Courts

To provide simple, speedy and inexpensive redressal of consumer grievances under this Act, a three tier quasi-judicial machinery, popularly known as consumer courts, at the national, state and district levels have been set up. These courts are designed to render free redressal to the consumer's disputes against any defective goods and deficient services which include unfair and restrictive trade practices.

National Consumer Disputes Redressal Commission known as **National Commission** is functioning at New Delhi. Each State has a Consumer Disputes Redressal Commissions known as the **State Commission.** Similarly, every district in the country has a Consumer Disputes Redressal Forum-known as the **District Forum.**

The provisions of this Act are in addition to and not in derogation of, the provisions of any other law for the time being in force.

RIGHT TO INFORMATION

Right to information act comes into force on the 12th October, 2005 (120th day of its enactment on 15th June, 2005). Some provisions have come into force with immediate effect viz. obligations of public authorities [S.4(1)], designation of Public Information Officers and Assistant Public Information Officers[S.5(1) and 5(2)], constitution of Central Information Commission (S.12 and 13), constitution of State Information Commission (S.15 and 16), non-applicability of the Act to Intelligence and Security Organizations (S.24) and power to make rules to carry out the provisions of the Act (S.27 and 28).

The Act extends to the whole of India except the State of Jammu and Kashmir. [S.(12)]

Information-Meaning

Information means any material in any form including records, documents, memos, e-mails, opinions, advices, press releases, circulars, orders, logbooks, contracts, reports, papers, samples, models, data material held in any electronic form and information relating to any private body which can be accessed by a public authority under any other law for the time being in force but does not include "file notings". [S.2(f)].

Meaning of "Right to Information'

It includes the right to -

(*i*) inspect works, documents, records.

(*ii*) take notes, extracts or certified copies of documents or records.

(*iii*) take certified samples of material.

(*iv*) obtain information in form of printouts, diskettes, floppies, tapes, video cassettes or in any other electronic mode or through printouts.[S.2(j)]

The following is exempt from disclosure [S.8)]

(*i*) information, disclosure of which would prejudicially affect the sovereignty and integrity of India, the security, strategic, scientific or economic interests of the State, relation with foreign State or lead to incitement of an offence

(*ii*) information which has been expressly forbidden to be published by any court of law or tribunal or the disclosure of which may constitute contempt of court;

(*iii*) information, the disclosure of which would cause a breach of privilege of Parliament or the State Legislature;

(*iv*) information including commercial confidence, trade secrets or intellectual property, the disclosure of which would harm the competitive position of a third party, unless the competent authority is satisfied that larger public interest warrants the disclosure of such information;

(*v*) information available to a person in his judicial relationship, unless the competent authority is satisfied that the larger public interest warrants the disclosure of such information;

(*vi*) information received in confidence from foreign Government;

(*vii*) information, the disclosure of which would endanger the life or physical safety of any person or identify the source of information or assistance given in confidence for law enforcement or security purposes;

(*viii*) information which would impede the process of investigation or apprehension or prosecution of offenders;

(*ix*) cabinet papers including records of deliberations of the Council of Ministers, Secretaries and other officers;

(*x*) information which relates to personal information the disclosure of which has no relationship to any public activity or interest, or which would cause unwarranted invasion of the privacy of the individual;

(*xi*) Not withstanding any of the exemptions listed above, a public authority may allow access to information, if public interest in disclosure outweighs the harm to the protected interests.

Only that part of the record which does not contain any information which is exempt from disclosure and which can reasonably be severed from any part that contains exempt information, may be provided. [S.10]

Who is excluded?

Central Intelligence and Security agencies specified in the Second Schedule like IB, R&AW, Directorate of Revenue Intelligence, Central Economic Intelligence Bureau, Directorate of Enforcement, Narcotics Control Bureau, Aviation Research Centre, Special Frontier Force, BSF, CRPF, ITBP, CISF, NSG, Assam Rifles, Special Service Bureau, Special Branch (CID), Andaman and Nicobar, The Crime Branch-CID-CB, Dadra and Nagar Haveli and Special Branch, Lakshadweep Police. Agencies specified by the State Governments through a Notification will also be excluded. The exclusion, however, is not absolute and these organizations have an obligation to provide information pertaining to allegations of corruption and human rights violations. Further, information relating to allegations of human rights valuations could be given but only with the approval of the Central or State Information Commission, as the case may be. [S.24)]

Application Procedure for requesting information

1. Apply in writing or through electronic means in English or Hindi or in the official language of the area, to the PIO (Public Information Officer), specifying the particulars of the information sought for.
2. Reason for seeking information are not required to be given;
3. Pay fees as may be prescribed (if not belonging to the below poverty line category).

The time limit to get the information

1. 30 days from the date of application.
2. 48 hours for information concerning the life or liberty of a person.
3. 5 days shall be added to the above response time, in case the application for information is given to Assistant Public Information Officer.
4. If the interests of a third party are involved then time limit will be 40 days (maximum period + time given to the party to make representation).

5. Failure to provide information within the specified period is a deemed refusal.

Fee for application

1. Application fees to be prescribed which must be reasonable.
2. If further fees are required, then the same must be intimated in writing with calculation details of how the figure was arrived at;
3. Applicant can seek review of the decision on fees charged by the PIO by applying to the appropriate Appellate Authority;
4. No fees will be charged from people living below the poverty line
5. Applicant must be provided information free of cost if the PIO fails to comply with the prescribed time limit.

Ground for rejection

1. If it is covered by exemption from disclosure. (S.8)
2. If it infringes copyright of any person other than the State. (S.9)

Central Information Commission

1. Central Information Commission to be constituted by the Central Government through a Gazette Notification.
2. Commission includes 1 Chief Information Commissioner (CIC) and not more than 10 Information Commissioners (IC) who will be appointed by the President of India.
3. Oath of Office will be administered by the President of India according to the form set out in the First Schedule.
4. Commission shall have its Headquarters in Delhi. Other offices may be established in other parts of the country with the approval of the Central Government.
5. Commission will exercise its powers without being subjected to directions by any other authority. (S.12)

Eligibility criteria and the process of appointment of Chief Information Commissioner/ Information Commissioners

Candidates for CIC/IC must be persons of eminence in public life with wide knowledge and experience in law, science and technology, social service, management, journalism, mass media or administration and governance.

1. CIC/IC shall not be a Member of Parliament or Member of the Legislature of any State or Union Territory. He shall not hold any other office of profit or connected with any political party or carrying on any business or pursuing any profession. (S.12)

2. Appointment Committee includes Prime Minister (Chair), Leader of the Opposition in the Lok Sabha and one Union Cabinet Minister to be nominated by the Prime Minister.

Term of office and other service conditions of IC

1. IC shall hold office for a term of five years from the date on which he enters upon his office or till he attains the age of sixty-five years, whichever is earlier and shall not be eligible for reappointment as IC.
2. Salary will be the same as that of the Election Commissioner. This will not be varied to the disadvantage of the IC during service.
3. IC is eligible for appointment as CIC but will not hold office for more than a total of five years including his/her term as IC. (S.13)

State Information Commission

The State Information Commission will be constituted by the State Government through a Gazette notification. It will have one State Chief Information Commissioner (SCIC) and not more than 10 State Information Commissioners (SIC) to be appointed by the Governor.

1. Oath of office will be administered by the Governor according to the form set out in the First Schedule.
2. The headquarters of the State Information Commission shall be at such place as the State Government may specify. Other offices may be established in other parts of the State with the approval of the State Government.
3. The Commission will exercise its powers without being subjected to any other authority.

Eligibility criterion and the process of appointment of StateChief Information Commissioner/State Information Commissioners

The Appointments Committee will be headed by the Chief Minister. Other members include the Leader of the Opposition in the Legislative Assembly and one Cabinet Minister nominated by the Chief Minister.

The qualifications for appointment as SCIC/SIC shall be the same as that for Central Commissioners.

The salary of the State Chief Information Commissioner will be the same as that of an Election Commissioner. The salary of the State Information Commissioner will be the same as that of the Chief Secretary of the State Government. (S.15)

Powers and functions of Information Commissions

1. The Central Information Commission/State Information Commission has a duty to receive complaints from any person—
   (*a*) who has not been able to submit an information request because a PIO has not been appointed ;
   (*b*) who has been refused information that was requested;
   (*c*) who has received no response to his/her information request within the specified time limits ;
   (*d*) who thinks the fees charged are unreasonable ;
   (*e*) who thinks information given is incomplete or false or misleading; and
   (*f*) any other matter relating to obtaining information under this law.
2. Power to order inquiry if there are reasonable grounds.
3. CIC/SCIC will have powers of Civil Court such as -
   (*a*) summoning and enforcing attendance of persons, compelling them to give oral or written evidence on oath and to produce documents or things;
   (*b*) requiring the discovery and inspection of documents;
   (*c*) receiving evidence on affidavit ;
   (*d*) requisitioning public records or copies from any court or office
   (*e*) issuing summons for examination of witnesses or documents
   (*f*) any other matter which may be prescribed.
4. All records covered by this law (including those covered by exemptions) must be given to CIC/SCIC during inquiry for examinations.
5. Power to secure compliance of its decisions from the Public Authority includes-
   (*a*) providing access to information in a particular form;
   (*b*) directing the public authority to appoint a PIO/APIO where none exists;
   (*c*) publishing information or categories of information;
   (*d*) making necessary changes to the practices relating to management, maintenance and destruction of records ;
   (*e*) enhancing training provision for officials on RTI;
   (*f*) seeking an annual report from the public authority on compliance with this law;

(*g*) require it to compensate for any loss or other detriment suffered by the applicant ;
(*h*) impose penalties under this law; or
(*i*) reject the application. (S.18 and S.19)

Reporting procedure

1. Central Information Commission will send an annual report to the Central Government on the implementation of the provisions of this law at the end of the year. The State Information Commission will send a report to the State Government.
2. Each Ministry has a duty to compile reports from its Public Authorities and send them to the Central Information Commission or State Information Commission, as the case may be.
3. Each report will contain details of number of requests received by each Public Authority, number of rejections and appeals, particulars of any disciplinary action taken, amount of fees and charges collected etc.
4. Central Government will table the Central Information Commission report before Parliament after the end of each year. The concerned State Government will table the report of the State Information Commission before the Vidhan Sabha (and the Vidhan Parishad wherever applicable). (S.25).

Central Government, State Governments and the Competent Authority as defined in S.2(e) are vested with powers to make rules to carry out the provisions of the Right to Information Act, 2005. (S.27 & S.28)

Role of Central/State Governments

1. Develop educational programmes for the public especially disadvantaged communities on RTI.
2. Encourage Public Authorities to participate in the development and organization of such programmes.
3. Promote timely dissemination of accurate information to the public.
4. Train officers and develop training materials.
5. Compile and disseminate a User Guide for the public in the respective official language.
6. Publish names, designation postal addresses and contact details of PIOs and other information such as notices regarding fees to be paid, remedies available in law if request is rejected etc. (S.26)

If any difficulty arises in giving effect to the provisions in the Act, the Central Government may, by Order published in the Official Gazette, make provisions necessary/expedient for removing the difficulty. (S.30)

"Public authority" -meaning

It means any authority or body or institution of self-government established or constituted: [S.2(h)]

* by or under the Constitution;
* by any other law made by Parliament;
* by any other law made by State Legislature;
* by notification issued or order made by the appropriate Government.and includes any—

(a) body owned, controlled or substantially financed

(b) non-Government organization substantially financed directly or indirectly by the appropriate Government.

Public Information Officers (PIOs)

PIOs are officers designated by the public authorities in all administrative units or offices under it to provide information to the citizens requesting for information under the Act. Any officer, whose assistance has been sought by the PIO for the proper discharge of his or her duties, shall render all assistance and for the purpose of contraventions of the provisions of this Act, such other officer shall be treated as a PIO.

The duties of a PIO

- ❑ PIO shall deal with requests from persons seeking information and where the request cannot be made in writing, to render reasonable assistance to the person to reduce the same in writing.
- ❑ If the information requested for is held by or its subject matter is closely connected with the function of another public authority, the PIO shall transfer, within 5 days, the request to that other public authority and inform the applicant immediately.
- ❑ PIO may seek the assistance of any other officer for the proper discharge of his/her duties.
- ❑ PIO, on receipt of a request, shall as expeditiously as possible, and in any case within 30 days of the receipt of the request, either provide the information on payment of such fee as may be prescribed or reject the request for any of the reasons specified in S.8 or S.9.
- ❑ Where the information requested for concerns the life or liberty of a person, the same shall be provided within forty-eight hours of the receipt of the request.

- If the PIO fails to give decision on the request within the period specified, he shall be deemed to have refused the request.
- Where a request has been rejected, the PIO shall communicate to the requester - (*i*) the reasons for such rejection, (*ii*) the period within which an appeal against such rejection may be preferred, and (*iii*) the particulars of the Appellate Authority.
- PIO shall provide information in the form in which it is sought unless it would disproportionately divert the resources of the Public Authority or would be detrimental to the safety or preservation of the record in question.
- If allowing partial access, the PIO shall give a notice to the applicant, informing:
  (*a*) that only part of the record requested, after severance of the record containing information which is exempt from disclosure, is being provided;
  (*b*) the reasons for the decision, including any findings on any material question of fact, referring to the material on which those findings were based;
  (*c*) the name and designation of the person giving the decision;
  (*d*) the details of the fees calculated by him or her and the amount of fee which the applicant is required to deposit; and
  (*e*) his or her rights with respect to review of the decision regarding non-disclosure of part of the information, the amount of fee charged or the form of access provided.

If information sought has been supplied by third party or is treated as confidential by that third party, the PIO shall give a written notice to the third party within 5 days from the receipt of the request and take its representation into consideration.

Third party must be given a chance to make a representation before the PIO within 10 days from the date of receipt of such notice.